Globalisation, Democracy and Corruption
An Indian Perspective

Globalisation, Democracy and Corruption
An Indian Perspective

Pranab Bardhan

frontpage

frontpage

www.frontpagepublications.com

First published 2015
Reprinted 2016, 2023

Frontpage Publications Limited
Level 2, 13 John Prince's Street, London W1G 0JR, United Kingdom

Frontpage
Level B, 76 B B Ganguly Street, Kolkata 700012, India

British Library Cataloguing in Publishing Data
A catalogue record for this book is available from the British Library

ISBN: 978 93 81043 17 2

Printed in India
By Sadhana Udyog
76 B B Ganguly Street, Kolkata 700012, India

Typeset by Compuset International
85 Park Street, Kolkata 700016, India

Contents

Preface

This volume is a collection of many of my op-ed articles, interviews and short essays on contemporary political and economic issues published originally in different newspapers and magazines in India and abroad.

These came out at different times over the last decade, and clearly and unmistakably bear the marks of the particular time when they came out. In each Chapter the date of publication is prominently displayed so that the reader can keep the date very much in mind while reading the piece, as many details and may have changed since then. My hope is topical context that the issues discussed retain their broad relevance, even though some details may not.

Since these pieces came out at different times and were meant for different audiences and readerships, there are some inevitable duplications, for which I seek the reader's forbearance. Deleting those duplications would have interfered with the flow of arguments in the respective pieces.

Also, as the primary readerships for the original pieces were in some cases Indian and in some other cases non-Indian, the degree of familiarity of Indian issues and events presumed has been different. The reader will note that in the pieces published in Indian newspapers and magazines a somewhat larger degree of familiarity with local issues has been presumed, but it should not be a major problem for the non-Indian reader to follow.

Most of the interviews published here are those that I gave to newspapers or magazines; only the last chapter is primarily my interview of Amartya Sen around two of his books.

Grateful acknowledgment is due to the editors at various outlets where the pieces originally came out for their generous permission to reprint and to Abhijit Mazumder for making the enormous effort in bringing out this volume.

Pranab Bardhan
Kolkata, February 2015

I

GLOBALISATION

CHAPTER 1

Does Globalisation Help or Hurt the World's Poor?

Scientific American, April 2006

Globalisation and the attendant concerns about poverty and inequality have become a focus of discussion in a way that few other topics, except for international terrorism or global warming, have. Most people I know have a strong opinion on globalisation and all of them express an interest in well-being of the world's poor. The financial press and influential international officials confidently assert that global free markets expand the horizons for the poor, whereas activist-protesters hold the opposite belief with equal intensity. Yet, the strength of people's conviction is often in inverse proportion to the amount of robust factual evidence they have.

As is common in contentious public debates, different people mean different things by the same word. Some interpret "Globalisation" to mean the global reach of communications technology and capital movements, some think of the outsourcing by domestic companies in rich countries, and others see globalisation as a byword for corporate capitalism or American cultural and economic hegemony. So, it is best to be clear at the outset of this article that I shall primarily refer to economic globalisation—the expansion of foreign trade and investment. How does this process affect the wages, incomes and access to resources for the poorest people in the world? This question is one of the most important issues in social science today.

For a quarter century after World War II, most developing countries in Africa, Asia and Latin America insulated their economies from the rest of the world. Since then, though, most have opened their markets. For instance, between 1980 and 2000, trade in goods and services expanded from 23 to 46 per cent of gross domestic product (GDP) in China and from 19 to 30 per cent in India. Such changes have caused many hardships for the poor in developing countries but have also created opportunities that some nations utilise and others do not, largely depending on their domestic political and economic institutions (The same is true for low wage workers in the US, although the effects of globalisation on rich countries are beyond the scope of this article). The net outcome is often quite complex and almost always context-dependent, belying the glib pronouncements for or against globalisation made in the opposing camps. Understanding the complexities is essential to taking effective action.

NEITHER PLAGUE NOR PANACEA

The case for free trade rests on the age-old principle of comparative advantage, the idea that countries are better off when they export the things they are best at producing, and import the rest. Most mainstream economists accept the principle, but even they have serious differences of opinion on the balance of potential benefits and actual costs from trade and on the importance of social protection for the poor. Free traders believe that the rising tide of international specialisation and investment lifts all boats. Others point out that many poor people lack the capacity to adjust, retool and relocate with changing market conditions. These scholars argue that benefits of specialisation materialise in the long run, over which people and resources are assumed to be fully mobile, whereas the adjustments can cause pain in the short run.

The debate among economists is a paragon of civility compared with the one taking place in the streets. Antiglobalisers' central claim is that globalisation is making the rich richer and the poor poorer; proglobalisers assert that it actually helps the poor. But if one looks at the factual evidence, the matter is rather more complicated. On the basis of household survey data collected by different agencies, the World Bank estimates the fraction of the population in developing countries that falls below the $1-a-day poverty line (at 1993 prices)—an admittedly crude but internationally comparable level. By this measure, extreme poverty is declining in the aggregate.

OVERVIEW: GLOBALISATION AND POVERTY

- The expansion of international trade and investment is one of the dominant trends of our time, but policymakers and advocates tend to discuss it without carefully examining the evidence available in social science.
- Because the modern era of globalisation has coincided with a sustained reduction in the proportion of people living in extreme poverty, one may conclude that globalisation, on the whole, is not making the poor poorer. Equally, it cannot, however, take much credit for the decrease in poverty, which in many cases preceded trade liberalisation.
- Countries that get the economic basics right—improving infrastructure, ensuring political stability, carrying out land reform, providing social safety nets, addressing market failures such as impeded access to credit—tend to succeed at reducing poverty. Although globalisation can help, it is only one factor among many.

The trend is particularly pronounced in East, South and South East Asia. Poverty has declined sharply in China, India and Indonesia—countries that have long been characterised by massive rural poverty and that together account for about half the total population of developing countries. Between 1981 and

2001, the percentage of rural people living on less than $1 a day decreased from 79 to 27 per cent in China, 63 to 42 per cent in India, and 55 to 11 per cent in Indonesia.

But although the poorest are not, on the whole, getting poorer, no one has yet convincingly demonstrated that improvements in their condition are mainly the result of globalisation. In China, the poverty trend could instead be attributed to internal factors such as the expansion of infrastructure, the massive 1978 land reforms (in which the Mao-era communes were disbanded), changes in grain procurement prices, and the relaxation of restrictions on rural-to-urban migration. In fact, a substantial part of the decline in poverty had already happened by the mid-1980s, before the big strides in foreign trade or investment. Of the more than 400 million Chinese lifted above the international poverty line between 1981 and 2001, three fourths got there by 1987.

Similarly, rural poverty reduction in India may be attributable to the spread of the Green Revolution in agriculture, government anti-poverty programmes and social movements—not the trade liberalisation of the 1990s. In Indonesia, the Green Revolution, macroeconomic policies, stabilisation of rice prices and massive investment in rural infrastructure played a substantial role in the large reduction of rural poverty. Of course, globalisation, by expanding employment in labour-intensive manufacturing, has helped to pull many Chinese and Indonesians out of poverty since the mid-1980s (though not yet as much in India, for various domestic institutional and policy reasons). But it is only one factor among many accounting for the economic advances of the past 25 years.

Those who are dubious of the benefits of globalisation point out that poverty has remained stubbornly high in sub-Saharan Africa. Between 1981 and 2001, the fraction of Africans living below the international poverty line increased from 42 to 47 per cent. But this deterioration appears to have less to do with globalisation than with unstable or failed political regimes. If anything, such instability reduced their extent of globalisation, as it scared off many foreign investors and traders. Volatile politics amplifies longer-term factors such as geographic isolation, disease, over dependence on a small number of export products, and the slow spread of the Green Revolution [see "Can Extreme Poverty Be Eliminated?" by Jeffrey D Sachs; *Scientific American*, September 2005].

SWEATSHOPS

Global market competition in general rewards people with initiative, skills, information and entrepreneurship in all countries. Poor people everywhere are handicapped by their lack of access to capital and opportunities to learn new skills. Workers in some developing countries—say, Mexico—are losing their jobs in labour-intensive manufacturing to their counterparts in Asia. At the same time, foreign investment has also brought new jobs. Overall, the effect appears to be a net improvement. In Mexico, low-wage poverty is declining in the regions that are more involved in the international economy than others—even controlling for the fact that skilled and enterprising people migrate to those regions, improving incomes there independently of what globalisation accomplishes. A recent study by Gordon H Hanson of the University of California, San Diego, which took into account only people born in a particular region (thus leaving out migrants), found that during the 1990s average incomes in the Mexican states most affected by globalisation increased 10 per cent more than those least affected.

In poor Asian economies, such as Bangladesh, Vietnam and Cambodia, large numbers of women now have work in garment export factories. Their wages are low by world standards but much higher than they would earn in alternative occupations. Advocates who worry about exploitative sweatshops have to appreciate the relative improvement in these women's conditions and status. An Oxfam report in 2002 quoted Rahana Chaudhuri, a 23-year old mother working in the garment industry in Bangladesh:

> This job is hard—and we are not treated fairly. The managers do not respect us, women. But life is much harder for those working outside. Back in my village, I would have less money. Outside of the factories, people selling things in the street or carrying bricks on building sites earn less than we do. There are few other options. Of course, I want better conditions. But for me this job means that my children will have enough to eat and that their lives can improve.

In 2001, Nalia Kabeer of the University of Sussex in England and Simeen Mahmud of the Bangladesh Institute of Development Studies did a survey of 1,322 women workers in Dhaka. They discovered that the average monthly income of workers in garment-export factories was 86 per cent above that of other wage workers living in the same slum neighbourhoods.

Another indication of this relative improvement can be gauged by what happens when such opportunities disappear. In 1993, anticipating a US ban on imports of products made using child labour, the garment industry in Bangladesh dismissed an estimated 50,000 children. UNICEF and local aid groups investigated what happened to them. About 10,000 children went back to school, but the rest ended up in much inferior occupations, including stone breaking and child prostitution. That does not excuse the appalling working conditions in the sweatshops, let alone the cases of forced or unsafe labour, but advocates must recognise the severely limited existing opportunities for the poor and the possible unintended consequences of "fair trade" policies.

THE LOCAL ROOTS OF POVERTY

Integration into the international economy brings not only opportunities but also problems. Even when new jobs are better than the old ones, the transition can be wrenching. Most poor countries provide very little effective social protection to help people who have lost their jobs and not yet found new ones. Moreover, vast numbers of the poor works on their own small farms or for household enterprises. The major constraints they usually face are domestic, such as lack of access to credit, poor infrastructure, venal government officials and insecure land rights. Weak states, unaccountable regimes, lopsided wealth distribution, and inept or corrupt politicians and bureaucrats often combine to block out the opportunities for the poor. Opening markets without relieving these domestic constraints forces people to compete with one hand tied behind their back. The result can be deepened poverty.

Conversely, opening the economy to trade and long-term capital flows need not make the poor worse off if appropriate domestic policies and institutions are in place—particularly to help shift production to more marketable goods and help workers enter new jobs.

Contrasting case studies of countries make this quite apparent. Although the island economies of Mauritius and Jamaica had similar per capita incomes in the early 1980s, their economic performance since then has diverged dramatically, with the former having better participatory institutions and rule of law and the latter mired in crime and violence. South Korea and the Philippines had similar per capita incomes in the early 1960s, but the Philippines languished in terms of political and economic institutions (especially because power and wealth were concentrated in a few hands), so it remains a developing country, while South Korea has joined the ranks of the developed. Botswana and Angola are two diamond-exporting countries in southern Africa, the former democratic and fast-growing, the latter ravaged by civil war and plunder.

The experiences of these and other countries demonstrate that antipoverty programmes need not be blocked by the forces of globalisation. There is no "race to the bottom" in which countries must abandon social programmes to keep up economically; in fact, social and economic goals can be mutually supportive. Land reform, expansion of credit and services for small producers, retraining and income support for displaced workers, public-works programmes for the unemployed, and provision of basic education and health can enhance the productivity of workers and farmers and thereby contribute to a country's global competitiveness. Such programmes may require a rethinking of budget priorities in those nations and a more accountable political and administrative framework, but the obstacles are largely domestic. Conversely, closing the economy to international trade does not reduce the power of the relevant vested interests: landlords, politicians and bureaucrats, and the rich who enjoy government subsidies. Thus, globalisation is not the main cause of developing countries' problems, contrary to the claim of critics of globalisation—just as globalisation is often not the main solution to these problems, contrary to the claim of overenthusiastic free traders.

What about the environment? Many conservationists argue that international integration encourages the overexploitation of fragile natural resources, such as forests and fisheries, damaging the livelihoods of the poor. A common charge against transnational companies is that they flock to poor countries with lax environmental standards. Anecdotes abound, but researchers have done very few statistical studies. One of the few, published in 2003 by Gunnar Eskeland of the World Bank and Ann Harrison of the University of California, Berkeley, considered Mexico, Morocco, Venezuela and Ivory Coast. It found very little evidence that companies chose to invest in these countries to shirk pollution abatement costs in rich countries; the single most important factor in determining the amount of investment was the size of the local market. Within a given industry, foreign plants tended to pollute less than their local peers.

Like persistent poverty, lax environmental standards are ultimately a domestic policy or institutional failure. A lack of well-defined or well-enforced property rights or regulation of common property resources often leads to their overuse.

Responding to pressure from powerful political lobbies, governments have deliberately kept down the prices of precious environmental resources: irrigation water in India, energy in Russia, timber concessions in Indonesia and the Philippines. The result, unsurprisingly, is resource depletion. To be sure, if a country opens its markets without dealing with these distortions, it can worsen the environmental problems.

WHEN TALK GIVES WAY TO ACTION

Fortunately, the two sides of them, globalisation debate are—slowly—developing some measure of agreement. In many areas, advocates in both camps see the potential for coordination among transnational companies, multilateral organisations, developing country governments and local aid groups on programmes to help the poor. Going beyond the contentious debates and building on the areas of emerging consensus and cooperation, international partnerships may be able to make a dent in the poverty that continues to oppress the lives of billions of people in the world. Here are some measures under discussion.

Capital Controls

The flow of international investment consists both of long term capital (such as equipment) and of speculative short-term capital (such as shares, bonds and currency). The latter, shifted at the click of a mouse, can stampede around the globe in herd like movements, causing massive damage to fragile economies. The Asian financial crisis of 1997 was an example. Following speculators' run on the Thai currency, the *Baht*, the poverty rate in rural Thailand jumped 50 per cent in just one year. In Indonesia, a mass withdrawal of short-term capital caused real wages in manufacturing to drop 44 per cent. Many economists (including those who otherwise support free trade) now see a need for some form of control over short-term capital flows, particularly if domestic financial institutions and banking standards are weak. It is widely believed that China, India and Malaysia escaped the brunt of the Asian financial crisis because of their stringent controls on capital flight. Economists still disagree, though, on what form such control should take and what effect it has on the cost of capital.

Reduced Protectionism

The major hurdle many poor countries face is not too much globalisation but too little. It is hard for the poor of the world to climb out of poverty when rich countries (as well as the poor ones themselves) restrict imports and subsidise their own farmers and manufacturers. The annual loss to developing countries as a group from agricultural tariffs and subsidies in rich countries is estimated to be $45 billion; their annual loss from trade barriers on textile and clothing is estimated to be $24 billion. The toll exceeds rich countries' foreign aid to poor countries. Of course, the loss is not equally distributed among poor countries. Some would benefit more than others if these import restrictions and subsidies were lifted.

Trust-Busting

Small exporters in poor nations often lack the marketing networks and brand names to make inroads into rich-country markets. Although transnational retail companies can help them, the margins and fees they charge are often very high. Restrictive business practices by these international middlemen are difficult to prove, but a great deal of circumstantial evidence exists. The international coffee market, for example, is dominated by four companies. In the early 1990s, the coffee earnings of exporting countries were about $12 billion, and retail sales were $30 billion. By 2002 retail sales had more than doubled, yet coffee-producing countries received about half their earnings of a decade earlier. The problem is not global markets but impeded access to those markets or depressed prices received by producers, as a result of the near-monopoly power enjoyed by a few retail firms. In certain industries, companies may actively collude to fix prices. Some economists have proposed an international antitrust investigation agency. Even if such an agency did not have much enforcement power, it could mobilise public opinion and strengthen the hands of antitrust agencies in developing countries. In addition, internationally approved quality-certification programmes can help poor-country products gain acceptance in global markets.

Social Programmes

Many economists argue that for trade to make a country better off, the government of that country may have to redistribute wealth and income to some extent, so that the winners from the policy of opening the economy share their gains with the losers. Of course, the phrase "to some extent" still leaves room for plenty of disagreement. Nevertheless, certain programmes stir fairly little controversy, such as assistance programmes to help workers cope with job losses and get retrained and redeployed.

Scholarships allowing poor parents to send their children to school have proved to be more effective at reducing child labour than banning imports of products.

Research

The Green Revolution played a major role in reducing poverty in Asia. New international private-public partnerships could help develop other products suitable for the poor (such as medicines, vaccines and crops). Under the current international patent regime, global pharmaceutical companies do not have much incentive to do costly research on diseases such as malaria and tuberculosis that kill millions of people in poor countries every year. But research collaborations are emerging among donor agencies, the World Health Organisation, groups such as Doctors Without Borders and private foundations such as the Bill & Melinda Gates Foundation.

Immigration Reform in Rich Countries

A programme to permit larger numbers of unskilled workers into rich countries as "guest workers" would do more to reduce world poverty than other forms of international integration, such as trade liberalisation, can. The current climate, however, is not very hospitable to this idea.

Simplistic anti-globalisation slogans or sermons on the unqualified benefits of free trade do not serve the cause of alleviating world poverty. An appreciation of the complexity of the issues and an active interweaving of domestic and international policies would be decidedly more fruitful.

CHAPTER 2

Globalisation and Inequality

YaleGlobal, 27 November 2012

Economic globalisation in the sense of expansion of foreign trade and investment is, of course, somewhat anaemic, reflecting the impact of global recession, although still vigorous in the sense of continuous international transmission of technology, information, ideas and social media.

In the world of politics and policymaking, a cold wind is blowing dimming earlier enthusiasm for global integration and market liberalisation. The Doha round of trade negotiations is moribund. Economic integration in Europe is in disarray. Not merely is the fuming against imports from China and immigrants from Mexico now a staple of American electoral politics, the populist anger in all countries, rich or poor, against the galloping rise in inequality is often directed at the dark forces of global intrusion and competition.

To economists, however, it is unclear how much of the rise in inequality within a country is due to foreign competition and how much to the inexorable forces of on-going technological progress which contribute to considerable churning in the labour markets in any case: Computers, robots and ATMs would have displaced secretaries, welders and bank-tellers, respectively, even in a trade-restricted regime. Such technology, by raising the demand for skilled and educated labour, turns the scale against the masses of unskilled workers. There are usually many other forces operating on the state of income or wealth distribution in a country. As economic growth itself raises the value of scarce resources like land, minerals, or oil and gas fields, those lucky to have ownership rights or enough political connections to influence public allocation in their favour, have large windfall gains from rental income, skewing the income distribution in a way that is not directly connected with globalisation. It has been estimated, for example, in India that of the total wealth of its 46 billionaires, in terms of US dollars, in 2012, 60 per cent is derived from what has been called "rent-thick" sectors, like real estate, construction and infrastructure.

Even in China, which globalised quickly, in three decades turning from one of the most egalitarian countries into one of the most unequal, it is not clear that globalisation is mainly responsible for this rise of inequality. If it were, one would have expected a larger rise in inequality in the globally more exposed coastal provinces than in the remote interior provinces, yet the data show that the rise has been more in the latter. To the extent the Chinese export success in the initial years has been in labour-intensive products, it contributed in fact to the large reduction in poverty. Global markets for labour-intensive products like garments have also enabled many young workers, mostly women, from poor families in Bangladesh, Cambodia or Vietnam to climb out of poverty.

In contrast, expansion of exports of mainly skill-intensive products in India, like pharmaceuticals or software, may have raised inequality. So the sectoral composition of production matters. Even without globalisation, the usual structural transformation of a developing country has a substantial impact on inequality. As poor agrarian countries move away from low productivity but the low-inequality agricultural sector to high productivity but the high-inequality manufacturing and services, aggregate inequality rises, largely independent of globalisation. In rich countries, the disproportionate development of the financial sector, helped by but not rooted in globalisation, has made a small number of people extremely wealthy. This inequality persists through their grip on politics with lobbying power and campaign finance. In China, some of the rumoured excessive wealth of "princelings" and other relatives of Communist Party officials is derived from private equity firms, apart from real estate. Also, the Chinese financial sector worsens income distribution by underpaying bank deposits from ordinary households and using that money for subsidised loans to business.

In general, the impact of globalisation on a country's inequality depends on the state of its mass education, physical infrastructure, and labour-market conditions and institutions. Education enables workers to be more flexible in adjusting to market demand across tasks and occupations. In Latin America, an area of traditionally high inequality, a surge in public secondary education over the last two decades has improved the skill level of poor workers; the wage gap with better-off workers has started shrinking, even in a period of trade expansion. According to World Bank estimates, inequality of opportunity is declining in some Latin American countries, partly helped no doubt by the successful conditional cash-transfer programmes, inducing poor children to continue schooling. Studies show that Latin America now spends a larger share of GDP on the poorest 20 per cent of children than the United States.

Better infrastructure like roads, railways, power and telecommunication enables the poor in remote rural or backward regions to share in gains from expanding jobs in the global sectors and may thus reduce regional and urban-rural inequalities, which constitute a major part of a developing country's overall inequality.

Domestic labour-market conditions also shape the way the workers adjust. For example, in India there is some evidence that workers in the low-productivity informal manufacturing sector bore much of the brunt of the increased market competition from trade liberalisation in manufacturing.

Many of these displaced workers may have then crowded into the non-traded sectors, usually self-employed service, and their conditions may have contributed to increased inequality in a country where the overwhelming majority of the workforce is informal. The relatively few organised workers in India are better situated than the informal workers, but the labour movement there is highly decentralised and fragmented, reducing collective-bargaining strength.

In the world market as a whole the advent of developing countries pushing exports of labour-intensive products has raised the effective global supply of labour, whereas the credible threat of capital to locate elsewhere—and outsource— has increased relative bargaining power of business and eroded viability and influence of labour unions, causing upward pressure on inequality. For a long time unions in rich countries enabled workers to share in the rent from market power of the companies, but with increased global competition such rental income declined. The share of immobile, usually unskilled, workers suffered a disproportionate decline, compared to that of internationally mobile capital.

Countries where labour unions are centralised and workers have a strong safety net of public welfare and job retraining, there is better bargaining by workers and less resistance to globalisation, as in Scandinavian countries, compared to US or India where labour unions are usually anti-globalisation, with decentralised labour movements and patchy safety nets. In some countries, globalisation may also lead to overexploitation of fragile local environmental resources—forests, fisheries, water and more—on which livelihoods of the rural poor depend. But administered under-pricing of some of these resources—like irrigation water in India, energy in Russia, timber concessions in Indonesia—is a major factor in resource depletion; domestic vested interests are often responsible for continuation of such damaging policies.

In general, globalisation can cause many hardships for poor people, but it also opens up opportunities which some countries can utilise and others do not, largely depending on their domestic political and economic institutions. The net outcome is often complex and almost always context-dependent. Serious obstacles to redistributive policies are often domestic—landlords, corrupt politicians and bureaucrats, and the currently subsidised rich—and closing the economy does not usually reduce the power of these interests.

All this means that globalisation is often not the main cause of our problems, contrary to critics' claims, just as globalisation is often not the main solution of our problems, contrary to the claim of some overenthusiastic free-traders.

CHAPTER 3

Blaming Globalisation

YaleGlobal, 15 October 2007

Economic inequality is on the rise around the world, and many analysts point their fingers at globalisation. Are they right?

Economic inequality has even hit Asia, a region long characterised by relatively low inequality. A report from the Asian Development Bank states that economic inequality now nears the levels of Latin America, a region long categorised by high inequality.

In particular, China, which two decades back was one of the most equal countries in the world, is now among the most unequal countries. Its Gini coefficient—a standard measure of inequality, with zero indicating no inequality and one extreme inequality—for income inequality has now surpassed that of the US. If current trends continue, China may soon reach that of high-inequality countries like Brazil, Mexico and Chile. Bear in mind, such measurements are based on household survey data—therefore, most surely underestimate true inequality as there is often large and increasing non-response to surveys from richer households.

The standard reaction in many circles to this phenomenon is that all this must be due to globalisation, as Asian countries in general, and China in particular, have had major global integration during the last two decades. Yes, it is true that when new opportunities open up, the already better-endowed may often be in a better position to utilise them, as well as better-equipped to cope with the cold blasts of increased market competition.

It is, however, not always clear that globalisation is the main force responsible for increased inequality. In fact, expansion of labour-intensive industrialisation, as has happened in China as the economy opened up, may have helped large numbers of workers. Also, the usual process of economic development involves a major restructuring of the economy, with people moving from agriculture, a sector with low inequality, to other sectors. It is also the case that inequality increased more rapidly in the interior provinces in China than in the more globally exposed coastal provinces. In any case, it is often statistically difficult to disentangle the effects of globalisation from those of the on-going forces of skill-biased technical progress, as with computers; structural and demographic changes; and macroeconomic policies.

The other reaction, usually on the opposite side, puts aside the issue of inequality and points to the wonders that globalisation has done to eliminate extreme poverty, once massive in the two Asian giants, China and India. With global integration of these two economies, it is pointed out that poverty has declined substantially in India and dramatically in China over the last quarter century.

This reaction is also not well-founded. While expansion of exports of labour-intensive manufacturing lifted many people out of poverty in China during the last decade (but not in India, where exports are still mainly skill and capital-intensive), the more important reason for the dramatic decline of poverty over the last three decades may actually lie elsewhere.

Estimates made at the World Bank suggest that two-thirds of the total decline in the numbers of poor people—below the admittedly crude poverty line of $1 a day per capita—in China between 1981 and 2004 already happened by the mid-1980s, before the big strides in foreign trade and investment in China during the 1990s and later. Much of the extreme poverty was concentrated in rural areas, and its large decline in the first half of the 1980s is perhaps mainly a result of the spurt in agricultural growth following de-collectivisation, egalitarian land reform and readjustment of farm procurement prices— mostly internal factors that had little to do with global integration.

In India, the latest survey data suggest that the rate of decline in poverty somewhat slowed for 1993-2005, the period of intensive opening of the economy, compared to the 1970s and 1980s, and that some child-health indicators, already dismal, have hardly improved in recent years. For example, the percentage of underweight children in India is much larger than in sub-Saharan Africa and has not changed much in the last decade or so. The growth in the agricultural sector, where much of the poverty is concentrated, has declined somewhat in the last decade, largely on account of the decline of public investment in areas like irrigation, which has little to do with globalisation.

The Indian pace of poverty reduction has been slower than China's not because growth has been much faster in China but because the growth rate reduces poverty in India less largely on account of inequalities in wealth—particularly land and education. Contrary to common perception, these inequalities are much higher in India than in China: The Gini coefficient of land distribution in rural India was 0.74 in 2003; the corresponding figure in China was 0.49 in 2002. India's educational inequality is one of the worst in the world. According to the *World Development Report 2006*, published by the World Bank, the Gini coefficient of the distribution of adult schooling years in the population around 2000 was 0.56 in India, which is not just higher than 0.37 in China, but higher than that of almost all Latin American countries.

Another part of the conventional wisdom in the media as well as in academia is how the rising inequality and the inequality-induced grievances, particularly in the left-behind rural areas, cloud the horizon for the future of the Chinese

polity and hence economic stability. Frequently cited evidence
of instability comes from Chinese police records, which suggest
that incidents of social unrest have multiplied nearly nine-fold
between 1994 and 2005. While the Chinese leadership is right
to be concerned about the inequalities, the conventional
wisdom in this matter is somewhat askew, as Harvard
sociologist Martin Whyte has pointed out. Data from a 2004
national representative survey in China by his team show that
the presumably disadvantaged people in the rural or remote
areas are not particularly upset by the rising inequality. This
may be because of the familiar "tunnel effect" in the inequality
literature. Those who see other people prospering remain
hopeful that their chance will come soon, much like drivers
in a tunnel, whose hopes rise when blocked traffic in the next
lane starts moving. This is particularly so with the relaxation
of restrictions on mobility from villages and improvement in
roads and transportation.

More than inequality, farmers are incensed by forcible land
acquisitions or toxic pollution, but these disturbances are as
yet localised. The Chinese leaders have succeeded in deflecting
the wrath towards corrupt local officials and in localising and
containing the rural unrest. Opinion surveys suggest that the
central leadership is still quite popular, while local officials are
not.

Paradoxically, the potential for unrest may be greater in the
currently-booming urban areas, where the real-estate bubble
could break. Global recession could ripple through the excess-
capacity industries and financially-shaky public banks. With
more internet-connected and vocal middle classes, a history
of massive worker layoffs and a large underclass of migrants,
urban unrest may be more difficult to contain.

Issues like globalisation, inequality, poverty and social
discontent are thus much more complicated than are allowed
in the standard accounts about China and India.

CHAPTER 4

Global Experts Still Need Local Knowledge

YaleGlobal, 12 December 2013

For quite some time the economic development profession has gone global in a rather grandiose way. Those quick with pronouncements on global development issues get the maximum attention, rise to the top of the profession, and may even get to hobnob with international celebrities and philanthro-capitalists.

The premium has been on finding global patterns in fighting poverty—in promoting comprehensive development strategies meant for a broad range of countries, with the Washington Consensus or alternatively the so-called Beijing Consensus— and pronouncing overarching policy judgments on the hot issues of the day on a global scale, including austerity or stimulus, free trade, capital flows, global inequality, migration, intellectual property rights, the development of NGO movement and the like. The World Bank, one of the largest outfits of development professionals, is now undertaking a radical organisational overhaul, aiming at "global practices", in a sweeping realignment of technical staff away from its traditional pools of regional or country expertise.

It is also commonly observed that international organisations now vie with one another in devising new global criteria for ranking countries—for example, the Human

Development Index, the Environmental Performance Index or the OECD Better Life Index for environment, the Transparency International Index for corruption and governance, the Business Climate Index, the Political Risk Map, the Freedom in the World Report, the Index of Economic Freedom, and so on. Politicians take these indices seriously enough to complain if their country goes down a few notches in the latest rankings. Some countries take offence if their ranking in the corruption index worsens, and some years back the Chinese government reportedly put pressure on the World Bank not to publicise findings on pollution indicators for Chinese cities.

These international rankings are, of course, based on whatever patchy data one can lay one's hands on for a whole range of countries—one data generator for a reputable international organisation once told me that, as the annual deadline approaches, the pressure on them to somehow fill as many cells as possible in the international data matrix in front of them is intense—blithely ignoring uneven quality and poor comparability of data across countries, and in some cases where the data are practically non-existent, the tabulators even feel compelled to extrapolate from data for other countries in the neighbourhood.

This general tendency to latch quickly on to global patterns as such data may reveal a change that has been going on for some decades in the academic development economics community. As the chief editor of its premier field journal, the *Journal of Development Economics*, I used to be inundated by submitted articles carrying out cross-country statistical exercises, which on the basis of easily downloadable data with single observations for each country, large or small— similar to the United Nations principle of "one country, one vote"—came to conclusions on historical and policy issues of supposedly wide generalisability. Then the fashion shifted to experimental case studies carried out in different parts of the world, evaluating impact of development interventions at the micro level, yielding general recipes for the good fight against global poverty. There are, of course, well-known limits to the validity of the generalisations based on such methods, but these do not usually deter passionate believers in the cause.

With the advance of such "global practices" what gets short shrift is the old-fashioned in-depth study into the historical-institutional contexts of particular areas that can give insights into political, social and economic processes that do not easily lend themselves to sweeping global generalities or to the building of a policy consensus named after some global city. The conceit of economics—over social anthropology, for example—has been its superior ability to unearth supposedly universalistic principles, either based on clever explorations of rationality, or even when humans are demonstrably irrational or weak-willed, on an understanding of the psychological patterns of systematic departures from rationality. Ambiguity, contingency, contextuality and local specificity are at a discount as they make global verdicts or one-size-fits-all policy judgments difficult. Area studies have fallen into disrepute in the social sciences in general, and especially among economists, even those with considerable local knowledge in particular countries, try very hard to avoid their identification as mere area specialists.

For example, one of the longstanding, sometimes acrimonious, debates in the development profession which relates to the efficacy of foreign aid. One group finds in massive foreign aid a way of removing misery from the lives of hundreds of millions of people in the world trapped in unfortunate geographical, disease and other circumstances, and the other group considers aid to corrupt or feckless regimes as "money down the rat hole" at worst, and a factor weakening state capacity for independent development at best. Ignore for a moment the fact that the aid debate gets exaggerated importance in the Western media as most programmes to fight poverty are funded out of a country's own local resources. Net official development assistance was about 1 per cent of total central government expenditure in

India in 2011; even in Africa, in Ghana, Kenya and Morocco, the fraction was less than one-third. Taking the whole of sub-Saharan Africa, official foreign assistance was less than 20 per cent of gross capital formation in 2011.

To take another example, when environmental issues are discussed in connection with development, the talk is usually in terms of the obviously important problem of global warming; far less attention is paid to the increasingly severe problems of degradation and depletion, independent of climate change, in the local commons—the forests, fisheries, grazing lands and the traditional irrigation systems, on which the daily livelihoods of the vast numbers of the rural poor in the world depend. In order to understand the modalities and pitfalls of community-level cooperation or collective action in mitigating these problems, one has to acquire a lot more local knowledge in numerous individual cases than what the global experts have time for. The problem has been accentuated in recent years by the leaders of the international NGO movement, where the latter sometimes bring their missionary zeal, considerable resources and preconceptions about the global generalities on capitalist development to weigh heavily on one side of a local debate over the commons—say against a dam or a mining or infrastructure project—without adequate consideration of the difficult trade-offs often involved, arising out of the conflicting interests of different sections of the local poor in individual cases.

It may be too much to say that like politics, all development is "local", but the time has come to point out that in the development profession, the pendulum has swung too much the other way.

CHAPTER 5

Economics to Blame for Global Financial Crisis?

Business Standard, 29 August 2009

Amidst all the blaming and shaming of Economics that is currently going on in the media in the context of the global economic crisis, I feel, as a veteran member of the profession, strangely guiltless. (I felt the same way many years back when I was teaching in Delhi. A housewife I met, on finding out that I am an economist, blamed me for the rising prices she faced on her grocery shopping.) In a recent op-ed piece (*Financial Times*, 5 August 2009), Robert Skidelsky referred to the British Queen's puzzle at the failure of economists in predicting the crisis, and then he went on to suggest ways of rebuilding the 'shamed subject'. A sensible economist like Skidelsky surely knows that most of the Economics discipline is much more complex, nuanced, and multifaceted than the wooden caricatures of the subject that the media (maybe even advisers to royalty) now denounce. Very few economists have ever claimed knowledge of the exact timing of a crisis, and in general economic forecasting has often been regarded in the profession as "making astrology respectable". Many notable economists have been pointing to the gathering clouds, saying (some of them quite noisily) for some years that the pattern and pace of debt-financed consumption in the US was unsustainable, and that the financial market was overreaching itself in the opacity of the risk packages it was pushing, though none of them gave an exact date or measure of the imminent financial storm. Many economists I know both in the US and abroad never displayed any trace of blind faith in self-regulating markets, even though they did and continue to value the important coordinating and disciplining functions of the market mechanism. In a world of imperfect information, expectational errors and herd behaviour, and uncertainty beyond measurable risks, many agreed that one should be cautious in applying the standard market principles to the financial market.

Yet the media and the policymakers often ignored the naysayers, played up the free market yahoos, and ascribed the doubts and heresies of the dissenters to the influence of ideology, from which they themselves were supposedly immune. The general public played along as no one wanted to be a spoilsport when the stock markets were booming and the housing markets were flush with liquidity. Now after the crisis, the ferocity of which shocked everybody, the same media are pointing fingers at the whole subject of Economics. Some are even blaming the tendency to build mathematical models in the profession (and Skidelsky concurs).

In good times as well as bad the media play up largely the part that has to do with macroeconomics. Economics has a thriving micro part, which while lacking the immediacy and stridency of business headlines, goes on studying how millions of individual decisions are made and what impact they have on the daily lives of people from America to Zambia; in recent years microeconomics, while not giving up any of its theoretical rigour, has turned more and more to empirical data and new ways of testing hypotheses. In macroeconomics, in the last quarter century or so there has been a healthy turn towards establishing micro-foundations of macroeconomics, basing it ultimately on decisions by individuals rather than on vaguely derived aggregates. But in taking this turn some economists resorted to a kind of hyper-rationality in individual decision-making and ignored informational traps and financial frictions. A whole host of other economists (particularly those specialising in the Economics of imperfect information and behavioural finance—fields by now well-established in Economics, and recognised by their own Nobel prizes) have been convincingly criticising this trend, pointing to human frailties (systematic departures from rationality) as well as asymmetries of information among the market participants. In this kind of critique, as in the received theories, economic analysis has sometimes involved complex models that have required mathematical abstractions. That some mindless applications, by hedge-fund whiz kids and other sharp operators of mathematical formulae in option pricing or in valuation of complex financial instruments have brought about disastrous results in financial markets does not detract from the general need for using abstract models in getting a grip on complex reality. A model often helps in thinking about and sorting out the essential from inessential aspects of the problem at hand, in puzzling out the implicit assumptions that we often make even in our best intuitive judgments, and in discovering unifying principles that can connect a mass of seemingly unrelated issues.

This is not to suggest that all is well with the way we teach and research in Economics. Our courses and research seminars are often steeped in a kind of technique fetishism, and marked by a deplorable oversight of history and systemic issues. The latter, for example, made many economists in their zeal for financial deregulation in the US oblivious of the corrupt influence of the financial oligarchy (described in vivid terms by Simon Johnson, the former chief economist of the IMF, in a widely noted article, 'The Quiet Coup', The Atlantic, May 2009). One can detect similar systemic obliviousness among the over-enthusiastic liberalisers in India of the corrupt grip of the industrial oligarchy in the political life of the country.

The complicity of the academia is reinforced by the fact that the beginning courses in major graduate schools of Economics in the US often succeed in weeding out students with lively minds still curious about general structural problems of an economy in the larger context of history and society, and mainly allow those who have the stamina and the manic perseverance to follow the current technical fads in their narrow groove. The premium is on cleverness, not on balanced judgment or wisdom. We can serve our profession (and the policy world) better if we do not take our findings and formulae too seriously or lose sight of the big picture, which historians and sociologists grapple with in a less precise, but often more insightful, fashion.

II

CAPITALISM

CHAPTER 1

Capitalism: One Size Does Not Fit All

YaleGlobal, 7 December 2006

A little over a decade ago the American model of capitalism was triumphant. The Soviet Union had recently collapsed, recession took the shine off the vaunted Japanese model of the 1980's, the social-democratic models of northern and western Europe languished in high unemployment and low growth, and the so-called East Asian miracle was soon to be engulfed in the Asian financial crisis. For many developing and transition economies in search of a model, there was only one prescription: Liberalise and privatise, and copy the Anglo-American institutions of legal, financial and corporate governance.

Today there is less certainty on the matter. First, the technology and then the housing booms in the US subsided; many years of high American living on borrowed Asian money are now widely considered unsustainable; extreme income concentration at the very top with stagnation at the bottom has made the hollowness of the productivity growth particularly palpable for most working people; unemployment in the US and the UK has been in general lower than in much of Europe, but their jails are full with a larger proportion of citizens incarcerated; and the crisis in health insurance and social security looms large. The earlier triumphal mood has now disappeared.

Meanwhile, the social-democratic and Japanese models, after some necessary repairs and on-going liberalising reforms, have come alive, with their economies revived, while still keeping a large part of their distinctive institutional features (These features will undergo some tinkering, but no substantial change, after the outcome of the recent Swedish elections).

Two of these features relate to the continuing emphasis on social protection and on a more coordinated style of corporate governance—in relations both across firms and between managers and workers. There is an increased appreciation of the fact that countries have different political contexts and the bargaining powers of the different stakeholders in the economic system—owners, managers and workers—vary. "One—Anglo-American—size fits all" is no longer the prevailing perception.

In the American system, the owners are dispersed and relatively weak, managers powerful and often overpaid, and employees not well-organised. This is not the case in much of Europe or Japan. This gives rise to a different sustainable pattern of corporate governance, even though there is more recognition now of the mounting costs of social protection, the need for more labour flexibility and protection of minority shareholders against insider abuse. Commentators have also pointed out that while the more open and competitive system in the US encourages radical innovations in technology, the more coordinated system in Europe and Japan is more conducive to incremental innovations, where workers on the shop-floor often contribute more to day-to-day technological improvements. Besides, the wage compression resulting from the more solidaristic wage-bargaining process, as in Nordic countries, helps the more productive firms at the frontier of technology at the expense of the less productive firms.

As for the developing countries, the East Asian model has not yet lost its influence. This model is characterised by initial relative equality, following upon land reforms and mass expansion of education, which helps in smoothing the wrenching conflicts and readjustments of early industrialisation. In addition, state-guided coordination of private enterprise and use of export performance to discipline firms strengthen, rather than stifle, the market processes.

The phenomenal growth of capitalism in China, with market reforms under pervasive government control—while starting from a position of relative income equality after the egalitarian land redistribution of 1978, providing a minimum safety net for most rural households—has only added to the attraction of the basic East Asian model. One-party rule Vietnam, opening its door to capitalist enterprises and growing at 8 per cent a year, offers a variation on the theme. India, another high-growth country in recent years, has also not quite followed the economic orthodoxy in a systematic manner, particularly in matters of privatisation, deregulation or fiscal deficit management.

In the 2006 Economic Freedom ranking of the Heritage Foundation, China and India rank far below most Latin American and many African countries. In these latter countries, which did follow the liberalising and privatising reforms of the Anglo-American model more faithfully during the last two decades, results in terms of economic performance have been, with a few exceptions, disappointing. Even the Bretton Woods institutions are now less confident in pushing their orthodox and austere "conditionalities" of loans in the cause of midwifing capitalism in the tropics—much like the declining confidence in foreign-policy circles for pushing democracy at gunpoint in the Muslim world.

Capitalism in both rich and poor countries has been afflicted by problems of rising inequality and environmental degradation. Globalisation has increased anxiety everywhere about job security. This underlines the value of social safety nets—and retraining facilities, portable health insurance and environmental safeguards—in coping with adjustments to market competition. The considerable opposition to globalisation, dismissed by most economists as populism, may be more a symptom of widespread disenchantment with the libertarian capitalism propagated since the Thatcher-Reagan era.

That era has, of course, left some healthy remnants. More attention is now paid in all countries to disincentive effects of state mandates, to the issue of individual responsibility in life decisions and to cost-effective ways of organising private provision of public services. There is also a greater appreciation of the wholesome effects of market discipline in cutting through much of the sloth, waste and malfeasance generated by years of reflexive interventionism. Of course, societies give different weights on economic efficiency as opposed to distributive equity and social harmony. The greater tolerance of inequality in American society reported in some surveys is not shared by other societies. In these other societies, the myth of high inter-generational mobility is less well-entrenched.

We need to explore the many ways in which equity can be enhanced without giving up on efficiency. These include expansion of facilities of education, training and health care. In many poor countries, the barriers faced by large numbers of people in credit markets, where they lack adequate assets that can be used as collateral, and land markets, where the landed oligarchy often hogs the endowments of land and water, sharply reduce the society's potential for productive investment, innovation and human-resource development. In societies with an extreme lack of equity, it is also more difficult to build consensus and organise collective action toward long-term reform and cooperative problem-solving efforts. Those who are preoccupied with these issues of social justice sometimes turn to various forms of anti-capitalism, as is evident in the environmental and anti-globalisation movements. But protest is not enough, it is necessary for these groups to explore viable, incentive-compatible and thus sustainable ways of constructing alternatives to capitalism. They have so far come up with few new constructive ideas, and history has not been kind to their old ideas.

On the other side, it is important to stress that single-minded pursuits of efficiency are bound to be counter-productive. In particular, a standardised policy prescription that ignores social and institutional diversities or the context-dependent complexities of a particular society is a recipe for failure. The accumulated resentment of the large numbers of losers worldwide in the process of globalisation—despite its theoretical potential of benefiting everyone—is already in danger of triggering a substantial backlash in many countries. The advocates of capitalism should try to protect it from the enthusiasts for any one particular variety of capitalism.

CHAPTER 2

Questioning Milton Friedman's Free Market and Freedom

YaleGlobal, 30 January 2007

Friedman met Pinochet in 1975 during a lecture tour to Chile, and critics of Friedman, unfairly charged him, a champion of freedom, with endorsing the military regime. What did soften him somewhat toward that regime was its eagerness to listen to the economic advice of the "Chicago boys" on the value of free markets. Beyond the ephemeral oddities of personal behaviour, there is a substantive issue worth pondering, particularly on the occasion of "Milton Friedman Day", celebrated on 29 January 2007.

Friedman openly gave primacy to economic freedom over political freedom. In his 1994 introduction to the 50th anniversary edition of Hayek's "Road to Serfdom", he categorically stated: "The free market is the only mechanism that has ever been discovered for achieving participatory democracy."

In this, Friedman seems to have gone beyond his line of thought expressed in the classic 1962 book, "Capitalism and Freedom" where he stated: "History suggests only that capitalism is a necessary condition for political freedom. Clearly it is not a sufficient condition."

Friedman's 1994 statement implies that economic freedom is a necessary and sufficient condition for political freedom. This important systemic issue in the transition paths of many developing countries today has not been adequately discussed. Take the two largest countries in the world, China and India. The last quarter century of history in China suggests that while there has been dramatic progress in economic freedom in the sense of expansion of market reform, it has not been sufficient to bring about a substantial expansion of political freedom. The first four decades of India after independence in 1947 show that a considerable amount of political freedom was quite compatible with what Friedman would consider large restrictions on economic freedom in the form of heavy bureaucratic regulations and control over the economy. (Many years back in a conference when Friedman attributed the widely-acclaimed post-war advance of the Japanese economy, in contrast to the relative stagnation of the Indian economy, to the regulations and controls in the latter, I pointed out to him that the Japanese state was not particularly a paragon of non-interference. His answer, unfalsifiable as it happened to be, was that the Japanese economy would have done even better without the state interference!)

It is possible that a quarter century is not long enough for the effects of economic freedom in China to work out in political liberalisation, and people point to other East Asian countries—South Korea, Taiwan—where capitalism, which thrived under initial decades of authoritarianism, may have paved the way for the eventual ushering in of democracy. But the police state in China shows no signs of loosening its grip soon, despite the dramatic progress in the opening of the economy. While there has been some relaxation in individual expressions of thought, the state never fails to clamp down on political activities that have even a remote chance of challenging the monopoly of power of the central authority. Some observers have even claimed that the large numbers of reported local disturbances in recent years in different parts of China—mainly around economic issues like land acquisitions, toxic pollution or mass lay-offs from state-owned enterprises—have allowed the central government to scapegoat and punish local officials, localise and diffuse unrest, identify discontented groups before they can coordinate across regions, and retain its tight control over the citizenry as a whole. Elsewhere in Asia, leaders in Singapore, poster boys of economic freedom in the eyes of many, have continued for decades to repress political freedom. Lee Kuan Yew's famed "Asian values" were market-friendly, but not very hospitable to political dissent.

In the Heritage Foundation ranking of countries in terms of their Economic Freedom Index for 2006, India's rank, even after a decade and half of market reform, is much below than that of Hong Kong, Singapore, Saudi Arabia, Kuwait, Cambodia, Kenya, Uganda and most of Latin American countries. Yet over several decades India has proved itself a vibrant, though unwieldy, democracy. Friedman sometimes made a distinction between political freedom and "human freedom". In terms of both, whether you take the well-known scores for political rights and civil liberties assigned by Freedom House, or the overall democracy scores given out by the Economist Intelligence Unit, India performs much better than those countries ranked far superior in economic freedom. Economic freedom does not seem to be a necessary condition for political freedom.

A look at the history of Western Europe does not clearly show that economic freedom, or "Manchester liberalism", brought about the victories of democracy. Theorists of democracy have often pointed to many other political or structural factors. For example, some ascribe the extensions of franchise and other democratic rights for the working class in the 19th century in Britain to the rivalry and conflicts between traditional aristocracy and the rising industrial bourgeoisie. Others suggest that democracy in Europe came as part of the political elite's strategy to prevent widespread social unrest. In mid-19th century France, Louis Napoleon shrewdly used the restoration of universal male suffrage to play the landed classes against the urban; he even reportedly advised the Prussian government in 1861 to extend universal suffrage, because "in this system the conservative rural population can vote down the liberals in cities".

In India it is arguable that the survival of political and human freedom, against all odds and at a time when government control over the economy was pervasive, had something to do with the fact that the elite was heterogeneous and fractured. No individual group could overpower others, and competitive politics provided a procedural device to keep the contending partners at the bargaining table within some moderate bounds. Democracy served as a resilient mechanism for conflict management in a highly divisive society.

Friedman in recent years had been quick to point out that intensive economic liberalisation in Pinochet's Chile eventually evolved into political liberalisation. But anyone familiar with the transition in Chile knows that the path was by no means smooth, and Pinochet tried his best to obstruct it. In any case, other countries have been far less successful in this evolution.

One mechanism for this evolution is supposed to work through the rise of the middle class. While economic liberalisation may strengthen the middle classes, these classes have not always been pro-democratic. Latin American or South European history has been replete with many instances of middle classes hailing a supreme caudillo. It is often the case that market reform tends to sharpen inequality. The resultant structures of political power, buttressed by corporate plutocrats and all-powerful lobbies, may hijack or corrupt the democratic political process, sometimes undermining the expansion of mass democratic rights, including the freedom of association of organised workers, and raise barriers to entry into the political arena for common people. Thus economic freedom may be important by itself, but neither necessary nor sufficient for political freedom.

CHAPTER 3

Capitalism as a Bogey

Hindustan Times, 31 July 2011

It has been reported in newspapers that in a recent public meeting in Delhi, CPI leader A B Bardhan (no relation) embarrassed his fellow leftist speakers, who were waxing eloquent about how 'neo-liberal' policies were responsible for increasing corruption in India, by pointing out that China also has a large amount of corruption. This suggests that there is a great deal of confusion and naïveté among people all around about the effect of 'neo-liberal' policies, and also about China.

Assuming that people are referring to the policies of market liberalisation when they use the catch-all (and intentionally derogatory) term 'neo-liberal', some people (including some neo-liberals) will claim that without such liberalisation the permit-control-inspector raj would have generated even more corruption—bureaucratic and political. Some leftists (though not the official ones represented in the meeting) may point out that it is hard to dispute that in market liberalisation China has gone much further ahead of India.

There may be an elementary confusion between correlation and causation here. Why does corruption appear to have gone up in a period of liberalisation? It is quite plausible that with high economic growth in both China and India, the market value of scarce public resources—land, oil and gas fields, mineral resources, telecommunication spectrum and more—has gone up enormously, and so has the chance of making money from their favoured allocation.

Second, in some sense there may not have been enough liberalisation. Despite great deals of deregulatory reforms and trade liberalisation, some major controls, particularly at the level of state governments, remain. For example, anyone who wants to start a factory needs land—often acquired from the State—water and electricity connections—made possible by relevant departments—and environmental and labour law clearance, putting the applicant at the mercy of the implementing agencies, and so on. This is not to suggest that some of these regulations do not have a rationale based on legitimate social objectives, but considerable official discretion is involved and, with that, some scope for corruption.

Third, over time, elections have become more expensive in terms of advertisement costs, fuel for transport, and alcohol and cash for the large numbers of vote-mobilising youth. Without public financing of elections, raising money from all kinds of private sources—often through illegitimate means—becomes indispensable. Of course, those private sources in turn demand and get *quid pro quo* from politicians in terms of policy favours.

While the third reason is obviously not operative in China, the first two are quite prevalent there as well. In fact, with fewer checks and balances either in government institutions or from independent judiciary, media or civil society, the corrupt in China can get away with unscrupulous behaviour much more easily. In rural areas, where households have user rights but not ownership rights on land, Chinese local officials, in collusion with local business, have been much more peremptory in acquiring land from farmers without adequate compensation. Nothing like India's recently enacted— though as yet weakly implemented—Right to Information Act (RTI) deters the corrupt Chinese official. There is, of course, the threat of severe punishment (including execution) for corruption in China. But such punishment is often arbitrary and, more often than not, used against political adversaries or small fry.

In the recent media splashes and leaks around the corruption scandals in India, showing the sticky fingers of corporate and real estate tycoons, lobbyists and journalists in good measure, the cosy nexus is usually described as crony capitalism. But such cronyism is actually more acute in China where successful State-owned and private-sector companies are often controlled by powerful political families. A report by the Chinese Academy of Social Sciences suggests that out of about 3,320 multi-millionaires (owning more than 100 million Yuans in 2007) among Chinese residents, more than 2,932 are relatives of high-ranking Party officials.

While there are hereditary political bosses and family business empires in India, there is also more vigorous competition in the private sector and quite a bit of churning in the list of top companies. India's crony capitalism does not approach the levels found in China. There are, however, grounds to believe that India has some institutional inducements for corruption that are weaker in China. First, in China, the lines of authority are more well-defined and streamlined whereas India operates with an administrative system of multiple veto powers on a given decision—a legacy of colonial times and distrust that is institutionalised in the administrative process. An apocryphal story has it that one high official in New Delhi told a friend, "If you want me to move a file faster, I am not sure I can help you, but if you want me to stop a file, I can do it immediately". In this system, even after paying a bribe, one cannot be sure if the job will get done, and payment may be required again.

Secondly, in China, official rewards and career promotions are more directly linked to local economic performance. Stealing so much as to adversely affect local economic growth can seriously hamper an official's chances of promotion.

In Indian civil administration, there are few rewards for enabling good local area economic performance; reputation for administrative efficiency does play some role in promotion, but seniority trumps most other factors in career paths. An official is posted in a given area for only a short period, plum postings often carry a price that the political boss does not forget to exact and so the corrupt official often has the incentive to squeeze the maximum out of the posting.

Of course, capitalism thrives on greed, which gets a premium in periods of high capitalist growth. But, on this matter, lack of liberalisation only gives expression to it in other forms, and in the matter of greed, Chinese businessmen do not suffer in comparison with their Indian counterparts.

CHAPTER 4

Chastened Capitalism Here to Stay

YaleGlobal, 3 April 2009

As the signs of a deep global recession proliferate, the tone of public commentators and editorial writers on the state of global capitalism is turning apocalyptic. As some question, are we witnessing the end of capitalism as we knew it? The speed and depth of the damage done in terms of loss of capital value, homes, and jobs as well as the magnitude of capital infusions and government stimuli boggle the mind. Some bemoan the possible demise of a system that in the last few decades produced unprecedented amounts of wealth and lifted many out of poverty in the far corners of the world. Others feel vindicated that after many years, their dire warnings of the risks associated with global capital concentrated in a few hands rang true. These dissenting voices hope that an alternative system, more just and less unstable and community-disrupting, will rise from the ashes.

While the search for such an alternative system that can combine justice and stability with sustained incentives for innovation and respect for individual human rights has eluded mankind for the better part of the last two centuries, one may be on firmer ground in predicting the emergence of only a somewhat modified form of global capitalism in the years to come. My crystal ball is just as cloudy as anybody else's:

No one knows if it will be a "lost decade" or a lost couple of years, but looking beyond the current storm in at least the medium run, certain features of change and in some cases lack of much change are likely to draw attention. Many people believe that the explosive growth of financial capitalism, way ahead of the real economy—global financial assets were more than three times the value of world output in recent years—will be somewhat tamed now. In the constant search of leverage and undervaluation, the introduction of a whole range of complex financial products and investment vehicles that enhanced the opacity of risk packages in the name of financial innovation will be slowed. There is a general outcry that for too many years the system has been hijacked by an overweening financial oligarchy that got away with compliant monetary policy, lax credit standards and crony credit-rating agencies. It is likely that there will now be a discernible movement back to producers from traders and arbitrageurs.

Despite widespread calls for greater international financial regulation, I do not, however, expect more than marginal tinkering, except some enhancement of resources at the disposal of the International Monetary Fund, some minor coordination in the case of banks owning foreign assets and some mild harmonisation of taxes. Most regulatory tightening is likely to be at the national level. At that level, the national diversity in the balance of power between industrial and financial capital, between management and large shareholders, and that between capital and labour will shape the variations in regulation.

The ramifications of the spectacular technological advance in communications and 24-hour trading in the financial world will linger; but most policymakers, not just the "born-again Keyenesians", will be wary in assuming that the market is sufficiently self-correcting in coping with those ramifications.

After the current panicky withdrawals of international capital subside, the basic asymmetry in international flows of capital and labour will persist—with substantially more constraints, cultural as well as legal, on labour. Hence, capital's threat of exit will remain more credible. This asymmetry will continue to weaken the bargaining power of labour, notwithstanding the muscle-flexing by American trade unions under a more friendly administration in Washington or the street demonstrations in Paris. The conflicting interests of skilled and unskilled workers will continue to weaken the union movement, whereas the recession may actually bring about more consolidation of capital, strengthening it further. The labour share in national income in most countries may not thus show much improvement, and this will particularly be the case if the nature of technological progress continues to be skill-biased.

As in all deep recessions the pressure for economic nationalism and trade protection will mount, but compared to the past it cannot go very far now. In the global production process with a long and complex international supply chain, there is no truly indigenous product left to protect, and with components coming from all over the world labels like "made in USA" have lost much of their meaning. Even unskilled workers may soon see that protectionism is like shooting oneself in the foot—if you restrict free trade, you may no longer have the components and materials on which to ply your own trade.

However, the demands for social protection of workers will strengthen, backed in many cases by domestic business interests competing with businesses in other countries that have more state-funded worker protection. We already see this happening in the changing support base for universal health care. The main structural constraint on the increased provision of social protection will be the battle of demography against technology—the ever-growing needs of an aging population against the surplus generated from the innovation capabilities of the young.

Capitalism (not necessarily in its Anglo-American form) will keep on thriving in China and India, though at a less frenzied pace in the immediate future. In any case, contrary to repeated assertions in the financial press, much of their high growth in the last quarter century has been driven by mainly domestic factors. Even at the height of global expansion of trade in the period 2002-07, the increase in net exports contributed only about 15 per cent of total real GDP growth in China in that period. Over the last year Chinese exports have fallen from their dizzying heights, and this has caused sizeable job losses in some coastal provinces. But much of the exports from China, as well as India, involve processing of imported materials, and so the net loss in value added is not as large as the gross export figures suggest; in value added terms the high Chinese export to GDP ratio in recent years was about half of the usually reported gross ratio.

Also, the jobs in the export sector have been relatively small in terms of the total size of the labour force in both countries, more so in China than in India. China also has lot more financial resources to boost consumer demand in the short run and strengthen the social safety net for workers and peasants in the long run. The near-universal healthcare announced as part of the stimulus programme, if implemented, will serve both of these goals. High savings in both China and India, not just their stringent regulations and government ownership of banks, have given them relative insulation from external financial contagion.

Smaller developing countries, more dependent on exports, foreign capital and remittances, will suffer much more. There may be increased political instability in some of these countries, as has been the case in earlier large macroeconomic shocks, but this will not make much of a dent in the global capitalist system.

Over more than a century, capitalism, with all its inequity, instability and immorality, has shown a remarkable resilience. Such resilience is likely to continue, but only if politics at the national level can tame capitalism's excesses and mobilise its surplus to strengthen social protection.

CHAPTER 5

Prospects of Capitalism in India

Outlook, 2 January 2012

Unlike capitalism in the West, Indian capitalism is not quite in dire crisis, even though there has been some perceptible decline in business confidence lately. The crisis in the West will, of course, adversely affect Indian exports and foreign investment, but the engine of growth in India remains largely domestic, the significant opening to globalisation in the last two decades notwithstanding.

Unlike the West, India has a large young population with a great, and as yet substantially untapped, potential for entrepreneurship and a relatively high savings rate with the prospects of funding such ventures. People praise Indian entrepreneurs' various design innovations and remarkable capacity for improvisation (*'jugad'*). But, in the realisation of the great potential, there are quite a few formidable roadblocks. One relates to the deficiencies of various ingredients of capitalist production in India and the other, at a deeper level, to the perceived legitimacy of capitalism in the eyes of the general public.

Capitalist production in manufacturing and high-valued services requires land, minerals, physical infrastructure (electricity, roads, railways, etc) and a skilled and healthy workforce as essential ingredients. In India, the current situation is fraught in all these respects. The issues of land acquisition and mineral extraction have become politically charged, as the farmers and *adivasis*, facing dispossession and eviction from ancestral land, long used to defrauding by contractors and middlemen and un-kept promises by politicians, have started agitating for a clearer recognition of their rights, better compensation, jobs, and relief from environmental despoliation.

Indian physical infrastructure is dismal for any modern semi-industrial economy. Electoral populism, keeping a lid on user fees, electricity and water prices, railway passenger fares (drawing cross-subsidies from commercial freight), and encouraging an atmosphere of giveaways, power theft and squandering of public resources with impunity make cost recovery difficult. These discourage investment (both private and public) in infrastructure. In particular, public investment in infrastructure (complementary with private investment) takes a long time to fructify and requires both short-run sacrifices in terms of budgetary allocation and purposive collective action. But the increasing social and political fragmentation in India (reflected in numerous caste-based and regional parties, sometimes playing pivotal roles in shaky coalition governments at the national level) often results in pandering to short-run particularistic demands in the form of handouts and subsidies, overriding coordination for the long haul. These handouts keep the fiscal deficit high, and the necessary government borrowing keeps the cost of capital high, which hurts finance for development.

On social infrastructure like education and health, particularly in quality more than in access, India's average status is worse than many developing countries. This stark and staggering fact cannot be hidden by the few stories of our bright IIT graduates earning fabulous salaries or those of successful IIM manager-entrepreneurs or first-rate hospitals (attracting medical tourism). Even in higher education, the quality of our universities is quite low by international standards; so is our spending on research and development that fuels innovation. At the level of mass education, the high rates of dropouts from secondary schools and lack of vocational training facilities make the Indian workforce particularly ill-suited to the demands of even semi-skilled labour in many occupations. In addition, chronic ill-health (for example, the world's largest anaemic or TB-infected population or malnourished children are in India) makes Indian workers extremely low in productivity. As a result, the competitive advantages of our low wages are often neutralised.

These constraints of land, labour and physical and social infrastructure handicap Indian capitalism even more than the usual horror stories about regulatory delays and official corruption that inevitably attend a new business proposal, particularly in some states, even after decades of economic liberalisation.

The second set of factors that undermines Indian capitalism is the more general issue of its perceived legitimacy in India's divided and unequal society. In spite of the great flowering of entrepreneurial energies in recent years, one cannot deny that there is a strong anti-capitalist (particularly anti-big-capital) streak in Indian political culture. This is not surprising in a country where "small people" (small and middle peasants, self-employed artisans and shopkeepers, bazaar merchants and petty middlemen, clerks, school teachers and service workers) constitute an overwhelming majority of the population, and their ranks are swelled by inexorable demographic pressure and by traditional inheritance practices and subdivision of property. The formal capitalist sector is involved in the work life of too few people (as it directly employs not more than two per cent of the Indian workforce), and while it does have some supply links with the informal sector, the major part of the latter is far removed from the capitalist domain.

In India, there is a deep suspicion (reflected in all political parties) of market competition that might lead to larger economic interests, often utilising their advantages of economies of scale, deeper pockets and better political connections, devouring small and localised business. Gandhiji had given sensitive and eloquent expression to this anti-market, anti-big-capital, small-is-beautiful populism and mobilised it in the freedom movement against the British. In recent decades, those bearing the legacy of the Gandhian moral critique of market expansion and competition have joined forces with those espousing the Left critique of capitalist exploitation of workers, peasants, and other small people and their rights over natural resources. They have built active grassroots movements in parts of the country for the protection of the environment and of traditional livelihoods, against the depredations of the capitalist oligarchy.

On top of all this, the high growth of recent years has brought about a significant rise in inequality in a country where the disparities in the distribution of land, education and social status were already high. At a time when, in spite of a great deal of government expenditure on anti-poverty programmes, the social safety net is still very patchy in a largely informal and rural society (and in remote areas often completely absent), the exigencies of ruthless market competition raise the level of anxiety for workers and peasants. Lack of education gives them very little flexibility in adapting to rapid changes in technology and markets. (Even among western countries, resistance to global market competition is stronger among workers in the US, where the social safety net is weaker, than in the contrasting case of the social democracies of Germany or Scandinavia.) In addition, the invidious inequalities and displays of newly acquired wealth (made more luridly visible in TV programmes) heighten the popular resentment at calls for market expansion and pro-capitalist reforms. National Election Studies data have shown that the majority of a large sample of respondents believes that reforms help mainly or only the rich. Accordingly, at election time, most political parties play down any commitment to reforms. A ruling party that introduces some reforms is quick to block them when in opposition. In Indian politics, inequality often leads to a kind of reactive, short-term populism which ultimately hurts both capitalist growth and pro-poor investments.

The long-run prospects of Indian capitalism, while not quite dismal, will require a great deal of structural and political changes to be sustainably bright.

III

INEQUALITY AND POVERTY

CHAPTER 1

More Unequal than Others

Project Syndicate, 1 December 2011

Inequality is on the public's mind almost everywhere nowadays. Indeed, in the world's two largest democracies, India and the United States, widespread popular movements against rising inequality and elite greed are becoming highly salient issues in looming national elections.

Yet, in both countries, some social inequalities have been on the decline over the last few decades. In India, certain historically disadvantaged groups (particularly among the lower castes) are now politically assertive. The most egregious vestiges of caste discrimination are gradually disappearing. Similarly, in the US, discrimination against women, African-Americans, Latinos, and homosexuals is declining.

These developments reflect a democratic advance in both countries. At the same time, however, the fabric of democracy is being torn apart by a staggering rise in economic inequality. Generally, economic inequality is easier to justify than racism and other forms of invidious discrimination. A fundamental tenet of American society is that everyone has an equal chance—a belief that appears more plausible with the decline of social bias. In India, this myth is less powerful, but there is a general feeling, shared even by some of the poor, that the rich deserve their wealth because of their merit, education, and skills.

There are two problems with this argument. First, education and skills are not inborn talents. The rich have access to better schools, health care, nutrition, and social support than the poor, which plays a decisive part in later academic and social success. Pre-school children in rich families have better nutrition, health care, and mentoring; there is evidence that much of the brain damage due to malnourishment for poor children may have already, irreversibly, happened by age three. When students from poor families start to fail in school, they have little or no access to remedial classes, whereas the rich receive expensive coaching from private tutors throughout their education. As a result, India has the world's largest number of school dropouts. Sociologists in the US have also documented adverse "neighbourhood effects" for poor children in inner cities. In Indian villages, where residential patterns are often even more segmented, such effects are acute.

The other problem in both countries is the rising importance of 'unearned incomes'. In India, as in other fast-growing economies, scarce public resources, such as land, minerals, oil and gas, and telecommunication spectrum, have shot up in market value recently, generating extremely high unearned income for the politically well-connected.

In the US, the deregulation of the financial sector over the last few decades, and the accompanying rise of dubious financial instruments, destabilised the real economy while doing little to improve productivity. The result, as everyone knows, was exorbitant financial gain for a select few, followed by large losses that were paid for by the many.

The US and Indian examples suggest that, in democratic societies, groups that promote social discrimination grow politically weaker over time. Economic inequality, on the other hand, is perpetuated through the politically powerful and well-funded lobbies of the rich. The trend is reinforced as elections become more expensive in both countries, leaving politicians increasingly dependent on contributions from wealthy donors who demand policies that are favourable to their interests.

This implies that anti-discrimination and egalitarian movements need to broaden their focus to include electoral reform, better financial regulation, transparent privatisation, and, above all, an overhaul of the education system to ensure high-quality schools for the poor and pre-school nutrition and health care. In addition, massive investment in both countries' creaking physical infrastructure would create jobs for some workers and improve the productivity of others

The advantages of improving education, creating more jobs, and increasing productivity seem clear. The question, then, remains why India and the US neglect both education for the poor and infrastructure. The answer lies partly in the fact that the rich in both countries are ceasing to use many public services. They send their children to elite private schools, are treated in expensive private hospitals, and live in gated communities where security and other services are provided privately.

Moreover, big companies nowadays have their own power plants, private roads, and many internal services as well. As the rich secede from the public infrastructure upon which the rest of society depends, it has become increasingly challenging to tax them in order to pay for services that they do not want or need. Meanwhile, the pre-existing countervailing institutions (like labour unions) for the workers get eroded by new technology and globalisation.

In India, greater social equality has meant that small numbers of hitherto subordinate social groups have begun to enter the political and economic elite. Once there, however, rather than trying to change conditions for the poor, they adopt the values of the elite while manipulating the symbols of identity politics—a tactic that still attracts votes. (Democratic South Africa shows how difficult it is to make a dent in economic apartheid.)

Both India and the US have responded to unrest over rising economic inequality with a kind of reactive populism. In India, this takes the form of loan waivers for distressed farmers (which weaken the banks); price controls for water, electricity, and public transportation (which wreck government budgets and undermine the prospect of long-term investment in those areas); and more subsidised food in the corrupt and inefficient public distribution system. Meanwhile, in the US, populist right-wing movements prefer tax cuts to long-term investment in infrastructure. At the other end of the political spectrum, anti-state anarchists cannot help in building institutions that will sustain pro-poor investments.

The world's two largest democracies face a grave economic challenge. They must find a way to channel the rising anger caused by economic inequality into productive investments that can make the rich feel that they have a stake in ameliorating conditions for the poor. If India and the US move towards overcoming the most pervasive inequalities, they will reinvigorate their democracies—and their economies.

CHAPTER 2

Time for India to Reduce Inequality

Financial Times, 7 August 2006

In the recent flurry of writings on the rise of India's economy, it is often said that economic inequality is far less widespread in India than in most other developing countries. For example, an article in *Foreign Affairs* on the "India model" claimed it is more "people-friendly" than most other development models, and that "inequality has increased much less in India than in other developing nations". On the Gini Index, a measure of income inequality on a scale of zero to 100, India scores 33, compared with 41 for the US, 45 for China and 59 for Brazil, the article notes.

Such accounts ignore the fact that the Gini Index for India is for consumption inequality, not income inequality. For most countries, consumption inequality is lower than income inequality, as the rich save more than the poor. India's National Sample Survey, a regular national survey of household expenditure, does not usually collect income distribution data, and the occasional alternative sources suggest a significantly higher Gini figure.

The survey does collect data on wealth. The Gini Index for asset distribution inequality in 2002 was 63 (out of 100) in rural India, and 66 in urban India; the corresponding figures for China were 39 and 47 respectively. These data do not, however, include ownership of human capital. In India, educational inequality—crudely measured as the Gini index of years of schooling in the adult population—is 56. This is not only much higher than in China (37), it is significantly higher than in most Latin American countries (Brazil is 39), and many African countries, not to speak of the US (which scores 13).

India's traditional caste system arguably makes it one of the world's most socially unequal countries. When one combines social and economic factors, India's inequality is at the higher end of the world scale. Does it matter for economic reform? I believe it does, because social heterogeneity and economic inequality make it difficult to build consensus and organise collective action towards long-term reform and co-operative problem-solving. When groups do not trust each other in sharing costs and benefits of long-run reform, there is the inevitable tendency to go for attainable, short-run subsidies and government handouts.

Reforms have been halting in India. In the National Election Survey for 2004, the largest social-scientific study on Indian elections, three-quarters of respondents with any opinion on the subject said that reforms benefit only the rich. Indeed, over the last decade, even ruling politicians who supported reforms have played them down during election time, and a party that initiated reforms has been quick to oppose them when out of power.

This duplicity is also evident within the left: in states where it is in power, its representatives are often too driven by the inexorable logic of fiscal near-bankruptcy and competition for investment to be pro-reform; but in New Delhi, their leaders regularly indulge in ideological grandstanding. Of course, opposition to reform is not confined to the left. Trade unions of the right as well as left-wing groups are opposed to privatisation and labour reform.

Severe educational inequality, for example, makes it hard for huge numbers of people to absorb shocks in the industrial labour market, since education and training provide some means to adapt to market changes. In China, the hardships of restructuring under a more intense process of global integration were mitigated by the fact that there was some kind of a minimum rural safety net, largely enabled by egalitarian distribution of land cultivation rights. In most parts of India, there is no similar rural safety net for the poor. So resistance to the competitive process that market reform entails is that much stiffer in India.

The discussion in India on economic reform is preoccupied with issues of fiscal and trade policy, financial markets and capital account convertibility. Reform would be more popular if it were equally concerned with the appalling governance of basic social and infrastructure services for the poor and with the need for greater transparency (recent attempts at backtracking on the new Right to Information Act, for example, do not bode well).

Opposition to economic reform thus reflects not just lingering nostalgia for old-style Fabian socialism. Without softening this opposition, Indian growth will remain hobbled in the global economy, contrary to the wishful thinking of the Indian elite and the expectations of the international media, blinded as they are by the triumphs of a part of the corporate sector which is as yet a tiny part of the Indian economy.

CHAPTER 3

Inequality of Opportunity: An Interview

Live Mint, 15 July 2011

Q: Since your old book on Indian political economy, what according to you is the new political economy in India, especially now when India is nearly a $2 trillion economy?

A: The political economy in India, in some sense, has changed; in some other sense, it has not. When I originally worked on it in the early 1980's, I have noted that there are certain groups, which seem to dominate policies. Now the composition of those groups has changed somewhat, yet the nature of what I called the dominant coalition has not fundamentally changed. Major change that has happened is that the corporate private capital sector is now much more important compared to some other elements of the coalition compared to say mid-1970s. The corporate coalition, particularly after economic reforms, has become (both) more prosperous and also more powerful, whereas the big farmer part of the coalition is somewhat less important—and sometimes it is also difficult to distinguish the big farmers and corporate interest because many of the big farmer families have now started businesses.

The other element of the coalition is the bureaucrat (class) that is weaker now, in the sense that because of reform we have fewer regulations, so bureaucrats have less power. On the other hand, the political class has not become less important. Over time, if anything, they have become much more important—the relation between the political class and corporates is much tighter now; all the stories about corruption and crony capitalism show that the relation is becoming much tighter than it used to be in the mid-70s.

Since then, however, the other part that has become important, which I think is a healthy thing, is that resistance has also become stronger. For example, the NGO movement, which was not very strong in the mid-70s say, is now much stronger. The media is also quite active, particularly electronic media, but not always for the good because quite often they sensationalise, but I think a lot more protests are now given voice through the media as well.

Q: Is not it counter-intuitive that liberalisation has not succeeded in disturbing this dominant coalition?

A: I do not think reform's objective was to dismantle the coalition; it was to facilitate deregulation. On this, the business coalition was divided. One section wanted reforms, the other was opposed to it; if you think about the Bombay club and others, they were not very enthusiastic about the opening up of the economy, etc. But over time, I think, much of the business sector has realised that India can take on the whole world. So the confidence of the business sector is much more today than it used to be 30 years back. (Economic) reforms cannot change the power structure. It deregulated (the economy) so that the bureaucracy's control over licences and permits has declined, but the corporate sector is more powerful. So the dominant coalition has not changed, but, of course, there is some rearrangement as I mentioned.

The other thing is over time as the economy has grown, certain resources became much more important than before. (For example) land, mines, minerals and telecom spectrum.

Why are they so important? These are sectors (where there is a) lot of money to be made. So there is a scramble for getting control over them. So you are talking about the mining mafia, land acquisition (conflicts); of course, we (already) know all about the scandals regarding telecom. These are sectors in which there have not been enough reforms; the latter were largely focused on trade policy and industrial policy. For example, there have not been much reforms on the way in which the mineral rights are allocated, telecom (spectrum) and land rights are allocated. Since land involves a very large number of people you hear big protests.

Q: The other data, which came out last Friday (8 July 2011), show that inequality has actually gone up. Is not this a matter of concern and why is it happening?

A: I think, in general, inequality is growing. Since poor people are not having enough jobs, but the economy is growing, what does it mean? Those who are not poor see their income growing and that is an obvious way of saying how inequality is growing. Agriculture productivity is low so those who are left in agriculture, their income is not growing fast. And others, who are not in the agriculture sector, say informal sectors like manufacturing or services, they are not having enough jobs, good jobs. Sometimes, unemployment is not a good indicator, because after all I cannot afford to be unemployed quite often, I have to get something, so I scrounge around in low productivity jobs. We do not have good jobs.

Q: The NSSO employment data show that the workforce is getting casualised.

A: I somehow think, and my view is shared by many now, NSSO (National Sample Survey Office), while it is a very good source of data, the survey does not represent the rich adequately. This is the problem in all countries and

India also; this under-representation of the rich is increasing, so I personally think NSSO data are not capturing the rise in inequality.

Q: You have, in the past, talked about the inequality of opportunity. Does not that worsen consumption inequality, particularly in a rapidly growing economy like India?

A: What does inequality of opportunity mean? If you are a girl born in an *Adivasi* family, look at your life chances and look at ours—completely different, so inequality of opportunity is extreme. Now in a country like ours, inequality of opportunity depends on three things primarily: One, inequality in distribution of land—how much land I have inherited by my family determines my future if you are in agriculture sector. Second, inequality of education, because for good jobs, I need education. Third, the inequality of social status, so an *Adivasi* or a *Dalit*: compared to a high or dominant caste, the situation is different.

In all these three respects, India is much more unequal than most countries of the world. Social inequality is very high, most people agree, so let me not go into that. Land inequality is extremely high, much higher than China. The other thing that surprised me, when I looked into the data, is how unequal is an opportunity to education. I looked into some data collected by World Bank for more than 100 countries, so they computed the inequality in number of years of schooling and I was shocked. I always thought Latin America is one of the world's (most) unequal regions, but inequality in education is much more in India. So, even if you do not have land, if you are not of high caste, the way to climb out of poverty is education; but if that is being blocked for so many people, no wonder, if you ask me, that India is one of the most unequal in terms of opportunity in the whole world.

Q: Can the present growth trajectory be sustained then?

A: The issue is political sustainability. When inequality grows like this, unrest, political troubles, corruption scandals will go on. But the problem is, when we protest, the alternative that we suggest is quite often populist. So whether in Gandhi caps (Anna Hazare) or red robes (Baba Ramdev), we are protesting (against) corruption, but giving populist suggestions. People like populist things, but quite often in the long run, it does not help. The problem with democracy is, it also encourages populism, which ultimately hurts the poor. I am worried about that aspect.

IV

DEMOCRACY

CHAPTER 1

Democratic Hysteria

Project Syndicate, 6 September 2011

In the political impasses of the mid-2011 that paralysed the world's two largest democracies, India and the US, both countries' usually clear-sighted leaders, to paraphrase William Butler Yeats, lacked all conviction, while the misguided and the shallow were full of passionate intensity. Indeed, that passion shows little sign of waning.

In the US, the economically illiterate, seeing misery all around from lost jobs, foreclosed homes, and the ever more apparent decline in America's international status, are distilling their frenzy from obsolete advocates of fiscal rectitude, while clutching their Bibles and espousing a juvenile understanding of the US Constitution. But their efforts are only digging a bigger hole for the US economy, making recovery much more difficult. Even their tax-averse sponsors, while appreciative of the rabble's efforts to protect their wealth, are now fearful of the impact of these wayward ideas on the investment climate and equity prices.

President Barack Obama, elected with a great deal of goodwill and hope in 2008, is now caught like a deer in the headlights. He knows that what the economy needs in the short run is different from what is required to be done to manage public debt in the long run, but he is unable to provide decisive leadership. His misguided efforts at compromise only fuel his opponents' frenzy.

In India, Prime Minister Manmohan Singh, who once enjoyed a strong reputation for integrity and intelligence, has been similarly paralysed, acting erratically in the face of an equally demagogic populist movement—the anti-graft crusade led by a fasting activist, Anna Hazare—which just ended in a frantic and uneasy compromise. Hazare, egged on by a flag-waving and indignant urban middle class and sensation-seeking media, tries mightily to claim Mahatma Gandhi's mantle; he is good at mimicking Gandhi's piety, but lacks his root wisdom.

Low-level corruption (the police, courts, and government clerks) has always been widespread in India. The type of corruption that has increased in recent years is partly a consequence of rapid economic growth. Public resources, like land, minerals, and hydrocarbons, and the telecommunications spectrum, have shot up in value, and in the scramble to control them, businessmen seek shortcuts.

Another reason for rising corruption is the soaring expense of elections, with politicians raising money from business as part of a *quid pro quo*. Both India and the US have little public financing of elections, and large business donations that are legal in the US are often illegal (and hence given underhandedly) in India. But, instead of addressing the structural causes of rising corruption, India's anti-graft movement bemoans a supposedly weakening of ethical values, and demands additional agencies with draconian powers to monitor and punish. The urban middle classes, impatient with the slow processes of democracy, latch onto holy men and their magic potions. Just as in the US, public rage is somehow directed away from the rich bribe-givers and onto venal politicians.

In both countries, the long-run implications of such angry populist movements for the health of democratic institutions need to be pondered. This is particularly true for India, where elections are vigorous and common people participate in them more enthusiastically than in the US, but other democratic institutions remain weak and sometimes dysfunctional, and the judiciary is too slow and occasionally corrupt.

To loud cheers from the crowds, the populists damn elected politicians as thieves and looters, but in the process disparage the institutions and processes of representative government. In the not-too-distant past, widespread denigration of this sort in Africa, Latin America, and other parts of South Asia often made it easier for populist authoritarianism to take hold.

Indeed, the widely heard slogan "Anna is India, India is Anna" reminds some of the dark days of Indira Gandhi's emergency rule in 1975-1977, when her followers raised the slogan of "Indira is India". But the slogan-mongers overlook India's extreme diversity. Many members of ethnic minorities, including the country's 150 million Muslims, openly oppose the Hazare movement.

One *Dalit* leader expressed his fear that Anna's success might inspire some majoritarian leader to rouse an even larger movement to rescind the protective rights and affirmative-action policies that have brought the lower castes some dignity. And some NGO leaders object that their own, very different anti-corruption agenda is being pre-empted by Hazare's demands.

In a populous country, it is not difficult to attract a large crowd. The electronic media are particularly attracted to colourful crowds waving flags and espousing nationalist causes. As one journalist pointed out, when 400,000 people (far more than Hazare's followers in Delhi) marched in Kolkata in May 1998 to protest against the government's nuclear tests, the media barely noticed.

Even when movements have near-universal support (which is not the case with the recent political movements in the US or India), there is a fundamental tension between democracy's procedural and participatory aspects. Apart from electoral reform, outlets for political participation and expression of public grievances must be balanced by institutions and procedures that are partly insulated from the rough-and-tumble of politics.

Of course, representative government does sometimes become unresponsive, particularly between elections, but direct democracy is not the solution. The US State of California, which has become increasingly dysfunctional since a 1978 popular referendum capped property taxes, can attest to that. Nor is it an answer to demand hasty enactment of legislation in the face of a threat to cause public disorder by starving oneself to death, as Anna Hazare has done.

Most citizens in the world's two largest democracies understand that democracy does not offer magic solutions. One of the most lamentable developments of our time is that so many are now prepared to try unhealthy palliatives and short cuts.

CHAPTER 2

A Plague on All Houses

YaleGlobal, 2 May 2012

As news of political intrigue, corruption and human rights abuse tumble out of a hitherto tightly managed Chinese system and as a slowdown in its frenzied growth rates seems likely in the near future, the triumphalist story of a "Beijing consensus" on authoritarian state-controlled capitalism looks a bit shabby now. But the other model practised in capitalist democracies, like the US and India, is looking wobbly, too.

Dysfunctional government and rising inequality have triggered a populism that bodes ill for both systems. The standard measures of income inequality, like the Gini coefficient is extremely high and increasing for China and the US. While India does not regularly collect income-distribution data, occasional estimates suggest an even higher value than in China. In social indicators for the poor, like basic health and education, India and the US are below what is average for their levels of income. The high fees charged in schools and hospitals in China have shut out many of the poor.

In China, populism takes the form of wallowing in nationalist glory and a form of nationalist petulance; the government tries to manipulate this in deflecting domestic criticism by pointing to an interventionist West and building wasteful "image projects". In India and the US, populism takes the form of short-term pandering by politicians.

Chinese authoritarianism has made it easy for the elite to convert political power into massive wealth and rampant crony capitalism—the 2011 Hurun Report estimates that the 70 richest members of the National People's Congress has a combined net worth of $90 Billion. There is evidence to believe that the too-big-to-fail state-owned companies and politically-connected private firms may have led to a serious misallocation of capital and blocked entry of new firms and exit of inefficient ones, spelling trouble for China's prospects of going beyond simple catch-up to the technology frontier. An atmosphere of tight control over a free flow of ideas and creativity will also curtail innovations. Without innovations, China cannot sustain its high rates of growth, as the artificially low prices of land and capital for politically favoured firms become difficult to maintain and the supply of cheap labour gets exhausted.

This is cold comfort for the world's democracies. Both India and the US, for example, are at the moment suffering from policy paralysis delivered by dysfunctional democracy. In both countries, a rising inequality has strengthened the forces of reactive short-horizon populism. In India, public resentment builds over corruption at high places as in the recent scandals over allocation of telecommunication spectrum, land and mining rights and over the economic and environmental depredations of the corporate oligarchy. Pressure rises for short-term populist palliative measures in the form of subsidies, handouts and loan waivers.

Even though these measures are taken in the name of the poor, the relatively rich grab most. For example, diesel subsidies meant for tractors and trucks end up going toward luxury cars of the rich, fertiliser subsidies mainly go to the wealthiest farmers, a large part of the food subsidy is diverted by middlemen and non-target groups, and more. The consequent budget deficits, now running up to 8 per cent of GDP, often hurt the cause of pro-poor long-term investments in physical infrastructure, including roads, railways or electricity, and in programmes of education, vocational training and health care. India's rickety infrastructure, both physical and social, hobbling its development, is a direct outcome of the democratic malaise of competitive populism.

In the US public anger over lost jobs and foreclosed homes is utilised by the rich to mobilise opinion for income tax cuts and against sensible energy prices or carbon taxes. Some conservatives keep on arguing, against all evidence, that an even lower tax burden on the rich is the key to promoting investment and growth. The budget crisis negates or postpones pro-poor investments, like those in the battered physical infrastructure and the ramshackle US institutions of health care and education.

Another fallout of dysfunctional democracy in both countries is increasing political fragmentation and refusal to compromise on the part of opposing parties. Collective action has always been difficult in India's extremely heterogeneous and conflict-ridden society. With the decline of the national parties that used to have some semblance of encompassing interests, their dependence on shaky coalitions at the centre, with regional parties and fiefdoms demanding accommodation for their special interests in constant day-to-day bargaining, comes at the expense of long-term policy consolidation. The opposition parties block reforms that they themselves advocated while in power. None of this is helped by pressure from outside the political parties. India's active NGO groups with their narrow single-interest agenda—for example, with hardly any compromise allowed on environmental and land issues where there could always exist some trade-offs. Problems of land acquisition and environment clearance have stalled many development projects.

In the US, also, political parties find gridlock for the cause of narrow ideological and special interests preferable to compromise for the long run, legislative filibusters, and other devices of checks and balances form a chokehold on major policy decisions. The Republican Party's congressional leadership and presumptive presidential candidate are hobbled by demands of no compromise by the social conservative base, not to mention their super-rich backers. The Democrats are tied by union and special-interest connections.

In both India and the US, the 24-hour media sensationalise, amplifying all conflicts, deflecting attention from a larger vision. It is high time both democracies pay some attention to devising new institutional mechanisms for insulating long-term decision-taking from the wheeling-dealing of everyday politics. For instance, the US could revise rules of filibuster and congressional committee functions. India could modify through various commitment devices the power of coalition partners in central government to threaten constant support withdrawal if their view is not fully accommodated. For example, a rule change, in line with an existing rule in Germany, has been suggested by which a no-confidence vote in Parliament should not be operative if confidence in an alternative government is not simultaneously affirmed.

Both countries need more independent regulatory and bipartisan policymaking bodies, with some power over the contours of long-run policy, with only periodic supervision or oversight by the clamorous legislatures. In both countries some attempts to increase public financing of elections and reduce the power of big money in funding political campaigns may alleviate the need of politicians to look constantly for funding sources and dance to the tune of special interests. In general, attempts to reduce the extreme economic inequalities may increase trust in government and make it easier to persuade most people to make short-run sacrifices for the long-run benefits of all.

Difficult though it is, doing something about inequality, corruption and political fragmentation, and installing some long-term commitment devices, may enormously help all political systems, democratic or otherwise. In particular, restoring trust in governance and some sense of fairness in the system of wealth distribution will be necessary if the political regimes in China, India and the US are to survive.

CHAPTER 3

What does this Authoritarian Moment mean for Developing Countries?

Financial Times, 22 August 2008

As the petro-authoritarianism of Russia flexes its muscles and the economic prowess of China struts in Olympic glory, developing countries in the world might start rethinking about the lectures on democracy and development that they have heard all these years from the West. This is at a time when advanced capitalist democracies are reeling under the shock of unregulated financial overreach and years of living beyond their means, a far cry from the end-of-history triumphalism of capitalist democracy of less than two decades back.

The Chinese case in particular is reviving a hoary myth of how particularly in the initial stages of economic development authoritarianism delivers much more than democracy. This is also backed by the memory of impressive economic performance of other East Asian authoritarian regimes (like those in South Korea and Taiwan in the recent past). The lingering hope of democrats had been that the middle classes prosper in these regimes, and in the latter two cases got as well, they then demand the movement toward political democracy. But the relationship between authoritarianism or democracy and development is not so simple. Authoritarianism is neither necessary nor sufficient for economic development.

That it is not necessary is illustrated not only by today's industrial democracies, but by scattered cases of recent development success: Costa Rica, Botswana, and now India. That it is not sufficient is amply evident from disastrous authoritarian regimes in Africa and elsewhere.

Even if we were not to value democracy for its own sake (or regard it as an integral part of development by definition), and look at it in a purely instrumental way, it is worth reiterating several advantages of democracy from the point of view of development. Democracies are better able to avoid catastrophic mistakes, (such as China's Great Leap Forward and the ensuing great famine that killed nearly 30 million people, or a massive mayhem in the form of Cultural Revolution), and have greater healing powers after difficult times. Democracies also experience more intense pressure to share the benefits of development among the people, thus making it sustainable, and provide more scope for popular movements against industrial fallout such as environmental degradation. In addition, they are better able to mitigate social inequalities (especially acute in India) that act as barriers to social and economic mobility and to the full development of individual potential. Finally, democratic open societies provide a better environment for nurturing the development of information and related technologies, a matter of some importance in the current knowledge-driven global economy. Intensive cyber-censorship in China may seriously limit future innovations in this area.

All that said, India's experience suggests that democracy can also hinder development in a number of ways. Competitive populism—short-run pandering and handouts to win elections—may hurt long-run investment, particularly in physical infrastructure, which is the key bottleneck for Indian development. Such political arrangements make it difficult, for example, to charge user fees for roads, electricity, and irrigation, discouraging investment in these areas, unlike in China where infrastructure companies charge full commercial rates.

Competitive populism also makes it difficult to carry out policy experimentation of the kind the Chinese excelled in: for example, it is harder to cut losses and retreat from a failed project in India, which, with its inevitable job losses and bailout pressures, has electoral consequences that discourage leaders from carrying out policy experimentation in the first place. Finally, democracy's slow decision-making processes can be costly in a world of fast-changing markets and technology.

The hopes of democrats relying on the middle classes in authoritarian regimes have not always borne fruit. Latin American or South European history has been replete with many episodes of middle classes hailing a supreme caudillo. The police state in China shows no signs of loosening its grip soon, despite the spectacular progress in the opening of the economy. While there has been some relaxation in controls over individual expressions of thought, and some open middle class grumbling over pollution and forcible acquisition of property, the state never fails to clamp down on political activities that have even a remote chance of appearing to challenge the monopoly of power of the central authority. Most people in the Chinese middle class are complicit in this in the name of preserving social stability, as long as opportunities for money-making and wallowing in nationalist pride keep on thriving.

So markets and capitalism will not do their political cleansing job automatically. On the contrary, markets often sharpen inequality, and the resultant structures of political power, buttressed by corporate plutocrats and all-powerful lobbies, may even hijack or corrupt the democratic political process, a phenomenon not unknown in some industrial democracies. Thus, both for democracy and development, other social forces and movements for civil and economic rights for the common people have to be pro-active and eternally vigilant.

V

CORRUPTION

CHAPTER 1

On Piety and Corruption

Outlook, 19 September 2011

Just as our society tends to latch on to holy men for miracle cures, the urban middle classes have placed great hopes on an anti-corruption movement led by a pious man in a Gandhi cap. (The other claim on leadership by a holy man in red robes did not quite pan out as intended.) The Anna Hazare movement wants to fight corruption with a new bureaucracy that will have drastic monitoring and prosecuting powers over politicians and officials. I will not comment here on the methods it has used to put the issue on the public agenda (including regular disparagement by Team Anna of institutions and practices of representative government), nor shall I comment on the wisdom of imposing a new super-agency (Jan Lokpal) on top of current institutions like the Central Vigilance Commission or laws like the Prevention of Corruption Act of 1988, without looking into the reasons why the latter have been relatively ineffective. I shall instead largely confine myself to the structural reasons for corruption which are not being dealt with and why merely tightening the punishment mechanism for bribe-takers may be woefully inadequate.

China has the severest punishment (execution) for those charged with corruption, after a trial that is usually summary. Yet, this has not much reduced the rampant corruption there.

If there is sufficient gain from a transaction for bribe-givers, they will find a way of tempting bribe-takers. In fact, when the risk of being caught and punished goes up, it is quite likely that bribe-givers will offer a risk premium to bribe-takers, leading to an increase in the size of bribe—quite a paradoxical result of having a more stringent punishing agency. It is curious that the Anna Hazare movement focuses more on venal bribe-taking politicians, not on their sometimes wealthier bribe-givers. One has seen quite a few businessmen and film stars in the cheering crowds. Of course, one can say that they pay bribes, but resent it. That depends on the type of corruption.

Corruption is primarily of two types: one is where bribe-givers pay money to speed up what officials are supposed to do as part of their regular duty; the other is where officials are paid to do what they are not supposed to do—for example, to look the other way when goods are smuggled, taxes are evaded, property value is under-assessed, driving licences and BPL or food ration cards are issued to unqualified people etc. The latter cases involve collusion between bribe-givers and bribe-takers to evade laws, and gains by both parties. Thus neither is likely to report this to investigators. It will be hard for many people in the urban middle class in India to honestly say that they have not been complicit in some collusion of this type. Chanting slogans in support of a pious man in front of TV is much easier.

One problem of successfully prosecuting corrupt officials is that it is difficult to legally distinguish, beyond reasonable doubt, between outcomes of simple ineptitude and dishonesty. Sometimes, small changes in administrative procedures work better than a super-bureaucracy (even apart from the ever-present questions of 'Who monitors the monitor?' or 'Will all members of the official Lokpal bureaucracy be incorruptible?' and so on). One such change is reducing the monopoly power of the official that the client has to face, wherever feasible. In the US, a citizen can get a passport from almost any post office, and so corruption in getting passports is much less than in countries like India, where the passport-issuing officer has a monopoly. Another case of reducing official monopoly power is from the historical examples of reducing corruption in the customs office in Singapore or the narcotics control section of the New York Police Department, by introducing overlapping jurisdictions of officers (in the latter case, for example, local, state and federal agencies had overlapping involvement in controlling illegal drugs, which used to be a major source of police corruption).

A less simple but important administrative reform is to change the current system of bureaucratic transfers and postings, which is a major source of illicit income of politicians in state secretariats. In general, career promotion for officers in India depends more on seniority than on performance, so an officer has the incentive to maximise his or her loot in the short period of a local posting before transfer. The Chinese governance system limits local official corruption by giving the local official more of a stake in the local economic performance. Chances of career promotion improve if the area under his jurisdiction grows faster. So even when he steals, he takes care, in his own self-interest, that the general economic performance of the area does not suffer.

What are the structural reasons that corruption may have increased in recent years? First, in some sense, the increasing corruption may be a consequence of India's recent success in high economic growth; with growth, the market value of scarce public resources—land, oil and gas fields, mineral resources, the telecommunication spectrum etc—has shot up, and so has the chance of making money from their favoured allocation by a public authority. Economists have thought about various imaginative auction mechanisms for such resources, whereby the public could benefit from getting the maximum surplus out of public resources.

Second, over time, elections at all levels have become far more expensive in terms of the cost of publicity, petrol for transport and alcohol and cash for the large numbers of youth hired to mobilise votes. Without public financing of elections, raising money from business sources, often through illegitimate means, is indispensable, of course, with *quid pro quo* deals in terms of policy favours. The activists hardly give enough emphasis on a whole package of necessary electoral reform, including public financing of elections, regular audit of accounts of political parties (here the bribe-taker is not an individual), disqualifying those with criminal charges from contesting elections (since this often leads to too many flimsy charges against political opponents and the cases go on dragging for many years in the clogged courts, this should be accompanied by special tribunals for fast clearance of such cases) etc.

Third, in the last two decades, there have been major policy changes, involving large transfers of funds from the central and state governments to various local-level programmes. For example, with decentralisation and devolution of authority to local sub-provincial governments, corruption may increase if proximity makes capture of local governments by the locally powerful people easier than in the case of higher-level authorities. Similarly, large sums of money are now spent in various anti-poverty programmes which, at the numerous local points of delivery, are difficult to monitor and audit.

Fourth, with the rise of hitherto subordinate social groups in political power, while this has in some sense deepened Indian democracy, the social churning may have had some adverse effects on the level of corruption. Let us point out at least two ways in which lower-caste emergence can contribute—and might have contributed—to more corruption. One is that aspiring low-caste persons, in their upward mobility, lacking the network and connections of upper-caste people, may use money as a substitute to climb their way up. The other is the fact that low-caste groups and other ethnic minorities often elect even corrupt leaders belonging to the same ethnic group, as issues of 'group dignity politics' trump other considerations. However, the history of south Indian politics, where such ethnic awakening happened in the early decades of the 20th century (much earlier than in north India), gives one some hope that, after the initial play of dignity politics wears off, voters start demanding more efficient and honest governance even from leaders of their same ethnic group.

One should also keep in mind that the perception of corruption often goes up in the public mind when a number of politicians and officials are arrested, and the system finally seems to be taking some remedial action, than in the days when they quietly got away with their misdeeds.

Paradoxically, the pervasive perception that everyone around is corrupt can sometimes actually increase corruption, as otherwise honest people yield to temptation more easily, since the chances of being individually detected are smaller, the expected reputation loss on detection is less important and the search cost for finding a briber is less.

Finally, overzealousness in erecting a corruption-detection machinery, for all the good intentions, can stifle honest and potentially beneficial but inherently risky decisions and dynamic leadership by public sector officials. If a risky decision does not work out, and somebody somewhere is seen to gain as a result, that often works as prima facie evidence of corrupt intent, and in anticipation, an official will often opt for less bold policies or status quo.

All this is to illustrate that corruption involves a set of complex and occasionally paradoxical issues that cannot be resolved by simplistic pious slogans.

CHAPTER 2

Our Corruption, their Corruption

Business Standard, 26 November 2009

In Chongqing, one of China's fastest-growing cities, the trial in a case of corruption against a billionaire Party official along with many of his associates and accomplices (public servants, judges, policemen and gangsters) brought to limelight the politician-business-criminal nexus, which is not unfamiliar to India. Corruption is pervasive in both countries, and in that context I have often been asked how, in spite of all the corruption, the Chinese economic performance has been so much better than India's. (Similar questions used to be asked of the phenomenal economic growth in South Korea and Taiwan since the 1960s, in the middle of their rampant corruption.)

Of course, in this matter, East Asia is not unique in history. In European history, the entrepreneurial class grew out of the sales of monopoly rights, tax farming and other forms of privileged access to public resources. In the US "gilded age" of late 19th century, the widespread corruption of state legislatures and city governments by business interests and those seeking franchises for public utilities has gone along with economic growth. But it is interesting to speculate on the several ways in which our corruption is qualitatively different from that in East Asia and on their differential economic effects.

First, in China the lines of authority are more well-defined and streamlined, whereas there is multiple veto power of different authorities on a given decision in India. An apocryphal story has it that one high official in New Delhi once told a friend: "If you want me to move a file faster, I am not sure I can help you; but if you want me to stop a file, I can do it immediately." So, even after paying bribes, one is never sure in India if the job will get done. This ability to "stop a file" at multiple points, part of a checks-and-balances system (originally installed by the colonial government suspicious of native officers, continued after Independence), acts as a damper on collusive corruption, but has ended up making our corruption rather dysfunctional. An offshoot of this system is institutionalised suspicion, which undermines incentives for bold decisions in the Indian bureaucracy. If a top bureaucrat does good work, the legitimate rewards are few, but if the decision leads to a project that fails, s/he will be hounded by the Central Vigilance Commission or the Central Bureau of Investigation (as it is often difficult for the latter to distinguish between decisions which simply did not work out and decisions which may have corrupt motivations). Thus the Indian civil service is highly risk averse and does not easily take innovative decisions. Institutional inertia rules, particularly because these officers, in any case, spend only two or three years on a given posting—why rock the boat?

Second, in China, official rewards and career promotions are more directly linked to local economic performance than in India, so the officials involved do not usually lose sight of the overall performance record, even as they line their own pockets. On my visits to Beijing, I have often privately asked my Chinese friends to give me their rough estimates of misappropriation of project value from the frenzied, large-scale public infrastructure programmes. None of these estimates exceeded 10 per cent.

I am reminded of another apocryphal story I once heard in Belgium that goes like this: In an international conference in Belgium, at the reception in the evening, an African minister took his host, a Belgian minister, aside and asked him how on his official salary he could afford to build the large mansion where the reception was being held. The Belgian minister took his African guest to the window and said, "See that road there? —10 per cent". Then, as usually happens in such stories, in a year or two, there was a similar conference in Africa where at the reception given by that African minister at his home, the Belgian minister asked how his host could build the huge palace on his income. The African minister took his Belgian guest to the window and said, "See that road?" The Belgian minister looked this way and that way, and said, "I don't see any road here". The African minister smiled and said, "100 per cent". I presume in China politicians do not steal 100 per cent, as their career promotion depends on the over-all economic performance of the area they are in charge of.

Third, in the past authoritarian regimes of South Korea and Taiwan, the political machine and its corruption were more centralised, which is less distortionary in its effects than decentralised corruption. Like the efficiency of "lump sum taxation" in public finance theory, lump-sum bribery distorts fewer decisions at the margin. Indonesia under Suharto was by most international measures more corrupt than India, and yet overall economic performance was much better. It is possible that Indonesian corruption at that time was more centralised (controlled largely by the first family and the top military leadership) and thus somewhat more predictable, whereas in India corruption was (and is) a more fragmented, often anarchic, system of bribery, as is now the case in post-Suharto Indonesia.

Finally, as elections become more expensive, politicians in India have to be on the lookout for serious money to an extent not necessary in China and other authoritarian regimes. Donations to election funds from the corporate oligarchy (and from real estate business), often under the table, have become more important. The corrupt impact of this on policy (including in matters of allocation of land, monopoly rights on natural resources or telecommunication spectrum or those of regularisation of all kinds of unauthorised constructions and environment-polluting enterprises) is much too evident. Of course, in this respect our corrupt election financing has brought about results that are similar to what Chinese authoritarian crony capitalism has achieved through unaccountable political processes. At least in India, one hopes, there are institutional processes and checks (through elections, courts, right to information, etc) in place which are somewhat more effective.

CHAPTER 3

Casteism and Corruption
Beyond Political Correctness

Ideas for India, 12 February 2013

Sociologist AshisNandy's remark that most corrupt people belong to lower castes drew a lot of flak. Here I comment on what I consider to be the two substantive issues coming out of this controversy—freedom of expression, and the corruptibility of historically disadvantaged groups.

Ashis Nandy has been a friend since my teenage days, so I was intrigued when recently some North Indian political leaders started baying for the arrest of this decent and humane scholar for his allegedly casteist remarks on corruption, until the Supreme Court mercifully intervened quickly to stop such nonsense. I want to discuss two of the substantive issues arising from this controversy.

But before that let me also state that I have found the remarks reportedly made by Nandy at the Jaipur literary gathering slightly convoluted in their strenuously contrarian position, and his subsequent 'clarifications' did not help. Some of his reported statements, like that about West Bengal, ruled for 100 years by upper-caste leaders, being relatively un-corrupt under CPI(M), is not merely subject to obvious misinterpretation about the implied honesty of upper-caste leaders, but is also generally false. West Bengal mid-level government functionaries, mostly upper-caste, have been no less corrupt than those in many other states. What is true is that the leaders at the very top in the more than three decades' rule in West Bengal by the Communist Parties have been, with some exceptions, relatively clean (though some of their relatives have not always been so), but that is by and large the case with Communist leaders in other parts of India as well, for reasons having to do with a history of party discipline, not their caste composition. But a careless statement by a public intellectual on the spur of the moment, while not uncommon and sometimes regrettable, is one thing and accusation of violation of an Act meant to prevent atrocities against minorities is absurdly another.

FREEDOM OF EXPRESSION—CONSTITUTION NOT ALL THAT LIBERAL

The first substantive issue is, of course, one of freedom of expression. I believe Nandy should have every right to say what he has reportedly said, even if I were to disagree with him. It is, of course, ironical that such liberal thoughts in his defence are usually associated with ideas flowing out of Western Enlightenment, which Nandy (along with his postmodern followers) had spent a lifetime of scholarship in deprecating. The liberals in India are, no doubt, aware that our Constitution (in upholding which the Supreme Court in its verdict has reminded Nandy that liberty should not be taken as a licence in public speeches) is not highly liberal on the question of freedom of expression. There are serious restrictions on free speech on grounds related to state security, public order, decency, morality etc. Any hoodlum belonging to some fanatic fringe can threaten about the potential 'offence' caused to his group, and even the faint possibility of the resultant disruption of 'public order' can get any book, film or art exhibition banned by the authorities. In recent years such acts of hostage-taking of our cowardly governments (both at the Centre and the states) have become an epidemic. In Indian democracy, group tyranny regularly tramples upon individual rights. In the name of preserving inter-community and inter-caste peace, we are now used to tolerating such tyranny, and the hoodlums thus win the day.

CORRUPTIBILITY OF HISTORICALLY DISADVANTAGED GROUPS

The other substantive issue is that of corruptibility of our historically disadvantaged low-caste and tribal groups. Even if people belonging to different groups have similar inherent propensities for honesty or dishonesty, different groups face different constraints, opportunities and pressures, and the 'equilibrium' outcomes may be different.

In the United States, suppose a white scholar notes the statistical fact that in crimes in metropolitan cities the incidence of involvement by blacks is larger than their demographic proportion in the population. Is he being necessarily racist? There is, of course, the institutional racism as a result of which the police and judicial authorities discriminate against blacks. But there are also socio-economic reasons like lack of opportunities and decent education and employment that drive many blacks to crime.

Similarly, in India there may be socio-economic reasons why in many cases the social minorities may be found to be involved in or supporting 'corrupt' activities, sometimes even more than the upper castes. Let me discuss two such reasons:

(a) One has to do with social networks (a point which I think Nandy was trying to make). The upper castes having been in positions of power and privilege for centuries have well-developed and well-oiled networks which their members can utilise in fixing problems or getting jobs and contracts for their relatives and friends. By and large the lower castes lack such lucrative and powerful networks. Under the circumstances, it is quite possible that an upwardly mobile lower-caste person may try to use money as a substitute for (the missing) network in getting things done. The latter will be called corruption, but the upper-caste use of connections instead of money for similar objectives is often not described as corruption. Is it 'casteist' to point this out? Lack of network may also mean that corrupt low-caste people get caught more often than equally dishonest but more protected upper-caste people.

(b) For social groups long subject to humiliation, it may be quite understandable that dignity politics often trump good governance. So it is often seen that a low-caste leader widely known as corrupt gets elected by his fellow caste-members, election after election, because these leaders in other ways have uplifted the self-esteem and dignity of whole groups of people. The leaders' corruption may even be looked upon with an indulgent eye: all these years the upper castes have looted public money, maybe it is now 'our turn'. Such symbolic group self-assertion in politics is quite prevalent in north India, where the rise of the historically subordinate groups is relatively recent. (In south India where self-respect movements are much older, good governance on the part of the low-caste leaders is more often in demand.)

In a survey of politician corruption in 102 legislative jurisdictions in Uttar Pradesh, where caste-based polarisation in voting behaviour increased between 1980 and 1996, Banerjee and Pande have shown a decline in the quality (in terms of competence and honesty) of the politicians who win. They find clear evidence of a trade-off between caste loyalty and quality of politicians.

Since stating these structural reasons in some way involves going beyond what Nandy has said, am I being even more 'offensive'? Some of Nandy's defenders have pleaded for him saying that he cannot be casteist, for after all he supports reservations for lower castes. Since I am not myself an unambiguous supporter of those reservations (I am for more substantial redistribution to the poor, but not necessarily through reservations), I do not have even that fig-leaf.

VI

INDIA–CHINA

CHAPTER 1

India and China
Governance Issues and Development

The Journal of Asian Studies, 12 May 2009

Any comparative study of contemporary China and India inevitably involves discussion of democracy and development, but most of the standard treatments stay at the level of simplistic clichés and high-minded platitudes. My goal here is to go beyond this, highlighting some of the complexities in the functioning of democracy in India and authoritarianism in China, and asking what this contrast tells us about governance and economic management in the context of development in these two large and still—despite record growth years—poor countries.

One reason such a consideration matters is that the dramatic economic success story of China in the last quarter century has revived a hoary myth: that authoritarianism delivers much more than democracy, particularly early on. This myth is reinforced by the memory of the impressive economic performances of other East Asian authoritarian regimes, such as South Korea and Taiwan prior to their democratic turns. The lingering hope of democrats has been that as the Chinese middle class prospers, its members will demand what their counterparts in South Korea and Taiwan got: movement toward political democracy.

The relationship between authoritarianism, democracy, and development, however, is not so simple. Authoritarianism is neither necessary nor sufficient for development. That it is not *necessary* is illustrated by today's industrial democracies and by scattered cases of development success: Costa Rica, Botswana, and now India. That it is not *sufficient* is evident from disastrous authoritarian regimes in Africa and elsewhere.

Even if we did not value democracy for its own sake, and looked at it in a purely instrumental way, it is worth reiterating some basic development-related advantages of democracy. First of all, democracies are better able to avoid catastrophic mistakes, such as China's Great Leap Forward (which was accompanied by a famine that killed nearly 30 million people) and the Cultural Revolution (which was linked to massive mayhem). Democracies also have greater healing powers after difficult times. In general, democracy provides a better capacity for managing conflicts, which in the long run enables a more stable political environment for development.

India's democratic pluralism has provided the means of containing many (though not all) social conflicts, a capacity that China's homogenising, monolithic state does not yet seem to have acquired. Faced with a public crisis or political shock, the Chinese leadership, which is otherwise so pragmatic, tends to overreact, suppresses information, and acts heavy-handedly. (One example of this heavy-handedness is that, according to some accounts by human rights organisations, although both countries have capital punishment, China executes more people in one week than India has put to death in the sixty-plus years since independence.)

Some degree of tolerance for diversity and dissent has historically been the safety valve for India's extremely heterogeneous society. For many centuries, on the contrary, Chinese authorities have typically given much less scope to pluralism and diversity; a centralising, authoritarian

Communist Party has carried on this tradition. Nurtured in this centralising tradition of control, there is a certain preoccupation in China (not just in the party) with order and stability and the importance of avoiding *da luan* (great turmoil), as well as a quickness to brand dissenting movements and local autonomy efforts as seditious. This often leads to unnecessarily harsh repression.

In recent years, China has diffused and contained many conflicts by localising them. More positively, the policy of decentralised development and regional autonomy has encouraged local initiatives and incentives. In order to keep these local initiatives under some moderate bounds and to make them serve national goals through tournament-like competition in regional economic performance, centralised control has been maintained through the channels of a promotion and reward system that encourages local officials to depend on those above them in the Party bureaucracy. But centralised control is not always benign, even though the Party leadership has in recent years curbed some of its arbitrary practices and shown some sensitivity to popular grievances. As long as checks and balances on the top leadership are not fully institutionalised, the danger of going off the rails in response to unexpected events and exaggeration of dissent always remains.

Democracies in general experience more intense pressure to share the benefits of development among the people, thus making it more sustainable. They also provide more scope for popular movements against capitalist excesses and environmental degradation. In addition, there are more political opportunities to mitigate social inequalities (especially acute in India) that act as barriers to socioeconomic mobility and to the full development of individual potential.

Finally, democratic societies provide better environments for nurturing the development of information technologies, a matter of importance in the current knowledge-driven global economy. Intensive cyber-censorship in China may seriously limit future innovation. Censorship (and anticipatory self-censorship) inhibits imaginativeness and inventiveness. State control of information also sometimes makes for delay in official recognition, and thus handling, of an incipient crisis. In China, from the SARS outbreak to last year's (2008) tainted milk scandal, there are many examples of this. Weeks before the latter scandal broke, journalists were encouraged to suppress bad news because of the Olympics, which was being stage-managed as China's moment of international glory. Journalists who were fully aware of the tainted milk case avoided writing about this "in order to be harmonious", as one editor said later (*New York Times*, 27 September 2008). Meanwhile, hundreds of thousands of children fell sick (a few even died), and the reputation of Chinese products was seriously damaged.

All that said, India's experience suggests that democracy can also hinder development in ways not usually considered by democracy enthusiasts. Competitive populism—short-run pandering and handouts to win elections—may hurt long-run investment, particularly in physical infrastructure, a key development-related bottleneck in India. Such political arrangements make it difficult, for example, to charge user fees for roads, electricity, and irrigation, discouraging investment in these areas. Conversely, in China, infrastructure companies can charge more commercial rates. Competitive populism also makes it difficult to carry out policy experimentation of the kind that China's leaders have excelled in throughout the reform era ("crossing the river, groping for the stones", as Deng Xiaoping famously put it). It is harder to cut losses and retreat from a failed project in India, which, with its inevitable job losses and bailout pressures, has electoral consequences that discourage leaders from policy experimentation in the first place.

In Indian democracy, the legislative process is often relegated to a second order of importance, giving short shrift to the deliberative process of democracy that John Stuart Mill and other classical liberal theorists valued so much. Overall, India's particular form of democracy relies less on deliberation than on popular mobilisation. This means that issues that could be resolved through the deliberative give-and-take get trapped in rhetorical intransigence and strident divisiveness of street theatre. Decision deadlocks are frequent, which has immense political and economic costs. This is over and above the general case that democracy's slow decision-making processes can be costly in a world of fast-changing markets and technology.

Besides, when democracy relies on popular mobilisation in a country where the general education level is low, civic associations relatively weak, and public debates relatively uninformed, the opposition can get away with being irresponsible (e.g., opposing the government for policies they themselves supported when in power). It also gives political opportunists leeway in segmenting the electorate along ethnic, regional, or religious lines; fomenting sectarian fear and anxiety is often a successful political mobilisation device.

The hopes of democrats relying on the middle classes in authoritarian regimes have not always borne fruit. Latin American and South European history has been replete with episodes of middle classes hailing a supreme caudillo. The police state in China shows no signs of loosening its grip, despite the spectacular progress in the opening of the economy. While there has been some relaxation in controls over individual expression and lifestyle, and more open middle-class grumbling over pollution and forcible acquisition of property, the state still never fails to clamp down on political activities that have even a remote chance of challenging the Party's monopoly on power. Many middle-class Chinese seem likely to remain complicit in this in the name of preserving social stability or "harmony", as long as opportunities for money making and wallowing in nationalist pride keep on thriving. A kind of preening nationalism has replaced socialism as the social glue in China, with the state leadership occasionally trying to stoke and then modulate collective passions about what the West or Japan had done in the past to China in the "century of humiliation" (sometimes fomented by frenzy on the Internet among the young) and to turn any external criticism into a slur on national self-respect.

The Indian urban middle classes also have a prickly nationalism, but more than harking back to two centuries of direct colonial subordination, it occasionally turns instead to majoritarian atavism to serve as a unifier in the context of unmanageable social and cultural diversity in society and works itself up questioning the national loyalty of domestic minority groups (in a context where the violent Partition of the country at independence remains a festering wound). Urban upper and middle classes in many parts of India are impatient about climbing the global ranks of big power and often regard as a hindrance and liability the numerically large poor outside their gated communities, with their all too visible squalor and messy democratic politics.

Democracy has brought about a kind of social revolution in India. It has spread out to the remote reaches of this far-flung country in ever-widening circles of political awareness and self-assertion among socially hitherto subordinate groups. These groups have increased faith in the efficacy of the political system, and they vigorously participate in larger numbers in the electoral process.

But the great puzzle of Indian democracy is why the poor, so assertive when election time comes, often do not punish politicians who are ineffective at resolving the endemic problems of poverty, disease, and illiteracy. It is possible that endemic poverty is widely regarded among the common people as a complex phenomenon with multiple causes, and they ascribe only limited responsibility to the government. The measures of government performance are in any case rather noisy, particularly so in a world of illiteracy and low levels of civic organisation and formal communication on public issues. A perceived slight in the speech of a political leader felt by a particular ethnic group will usually cause much more of an uproar than the same leader's failure to change policies that help keep thousands of children severely malnourished in the same ethnic group. The same issue of group dignity comes up in the case of reservation of public-sector jobs for backward groups, which fervently catches their public imagination, even though objectively the overwhelming majority of the people in these groups have no chance of ever landing those jobs, as they and their children largely drop out of school by the fifth grade. Even when these public job quotas mainly help the tiny elite in backward groups, as a symbol and a possible object of aspiration for their children, they ostensibly serve a valuable function in attempts at group upliftment.

While the electorate does not seem to penalise politicians for their endemic poverty, they are less forgiving when there is a sharp and concentrated deterioration in their economic condition. Amartya Sen has commented on the political sensitivity of democracies to the threat of famine, but to me, the more commonplace example for this in India is the electorate's high degree of inflation sensitivity. It is a common presumption that an annual inflation rate at the double-digit level, if it continues for some time, will be politically intolerable in India, and politicians universally support a conservative monetary and sometimes even fiscal policy to avoid this danger. The poor tend to make the government directly responsible for inflation and expect it to stop it in its tracks, even at the expense of cutting budgetary programmes for infrastructure that would help the poor in the long run.

The Indian electorate is often regarded as reflexively anti-incumbent, particularly in contrast with the electorate in the United States. This may have something to do with widespread dissatisfaction with the delivery of social services and public goods. Because the poor usually get mobilised along caste and ethnic lines, the modalities of such mobilisation are often multidimensional, and poverty alleviation is only one of many issues that get articulated in the public domain. Also, the process of ethnic mobilisation is often easily hijacked by the elite of these groups, who channel the lion's share of the benefits toward themselves. The intended poor beneficiaries are often unorganised and uninformed about their entitlements, and they also lack the ability to evaluate the quality of the particular education or health service provided.

Besides, at any given moment in India, an election somewhere is not far off (national, state, municipal, and village elections are staggered), and, as in election times everywhere, short-term calculations dominate. Populist quick-fix policies rather than sustainable improvements in structural conditions become the order of the day, and because it is usually the case in India's extremely fractious society that no disadvantaged group by itself is numerically predominant, the exigencies of electoral alliances with other groups (some of them not so disadvantaged) dilute the need to attend to the poorest. Because the better-off people (including better-off sections of disadvantaged groups) increasingly turn to private sources of public services (primary and secondary education, health care, irrigation, drinking water, child nutrition), the political support structure for public access to these services or improvement in their quality is rather weak or eroded in many parts of the country. There are also differential degrees of public vigilance over (or effectiveness of) different types of antipoverty programmes. Political clientelism prevails, under which the delivery of private and short-run benefits (in the form of temporary employment projects, subsidies, loan waivers, etc) get priority over public services and long-term investment in infrastructural facilities (roads, public health and sanitation, watershed development, etc).

The problem of poor delivery of social services involves more than just a lack of public vigilance or demand. It is a serious governance problem from the supply side as well (such as inadequate school buildings or health clinics with appropriate facilities and within manageable distance, rampant absenteeism by teachers, doctors, nurses, etc).

Decentralisation of governance in the sense of devolution of power to elected local governments was constitutionally adopted in India in the early 1990s. It was supposed to increase the accountability of the service bureaucracy as well as generate resources to address felt needs at the local level. But this particular governance reform remains largely on paper, except in three or four states, and in this sense local democracy is still rather weak in India. In most cases, local government officials are primarily involved in selecting the beneficiaries of programmes that are designed and funded from above. A large number of local governments simply do not have adequate funds, or the appropriate delegated functions or competent functionaries, to carry out locally initiated autonomous projects that could make a significant difference in the lives of the poor; there is considerable misappropriation of funds and delivery of services to non-target groups, sometimes giving decentralisation a bad name. Yet there have been some localised success stories.

In China, decentralisation has been successful in providing incentives (and discipline) for rural industrialisation. But decentralisation has increased regional inequalities. In spite of the fiscal recentralisation of the mid-1990s and a great deal of central transfers to local areas, there is a widespread rural budget crisis in China. The system is still sufficiently fiscally decentralised, with large numbers of unfunded mandates for local governments, that while the better-off regions can afford superior public services, the lagging regions have to live with large cuts in community services. These tensions of fiscal federalism are increasing in India, too. The better-performing state governments are now openly protesting large redistributive transfers to laggard states ordained by the Finance Commission. In the Indian democratic system, however, some of these laggard populous states (such as Uttar Pradesh or Bihar) send a very large number of members to Parliament, and the (shaky) coalition governments at the centre can ill afford to alienate them.

There are interesting contrasts in the style and content of governance in China and India. In China, there is more decisive policy initiative and execution than in India. This is not all attributable to an authoritarian setup. In general, collective action problems in goal formulation and policy enforcement are less severe in China than in the conflict-ridden, extremely heterogeneous society of India, where any major controversial decision is preceded by endless discussion, loud agitation, breast-beating street antics, and sometimes even fistfights and property damage; ultimately, what gets carried out after considerable delay is a much fought over, imperfect compromise. But for the same reason, executive authority in India, while weak, is more legitimate. The same disorderly processes of fractious pluralistic democracy that make decisiveness on the part of the leadership difficult also make executive authority more legitimate in the eyes of the people. The Chinese leadership, conversely, has to derive popular legitimacy from ensuring rapid economic growth and job expansion (which are under stress in the current recession), and also somewhat from advancing toward "harmonious" goals (i.e., environmentally friendly growth with some rudimentary social protection and effective political order). Ethnicity-based dignity politics, group upliftment, and other sectarian issues that crowd the political agenda in India are less of an encumbrance.

Recently, the Chinese political leadership has been more technocratic and professional than that in India, which helps in informed, purposive decision making. (Even the Party membership composition in China has changed substantially late: In 1978, two-thirds of the members were workers and peasants, but by 2005, their share had fallen to 29 per cent, and by then, 23 per cent of members were professionals, 30 per cent college students.)

Promotions in the administrative services are more performance based (instead of being seniority based) in China than in India. "Transfers and postings" of officials are major preoccupations of (and sometimes a source of illicit income for) Indian politicians, particularly at the state level. Rotation and temporary sojourns of Indian bureaucrats in a given job inhibit on-the-job learning of increasingly complex tasks. Regulatory effectiveness in commercial transactions is also better in China than in India, even though *guanxi* and corruption continue to contaminate the process. Nepotism in state appointments, however, may have gone further in China than in India. It is reported that many of the senior positions in some of the state-dominated sectors in China are filled by the children and other relatives of high-ranking Party officials. Some Chinese economists have warned about the dangers of crony capitalism.

Corruption is pervasive in both countries. But corruption in China is, in general, qualitatively different from that in India in at least three ways: (1) The lines of authority are more well defined and streamlined, whereas in India, there is multiple veto power of different authorities (part of the checks-and-balances system) on a given decision—as a result, even after paying bribes, one is never sure whether the job will get done. (2) Because the official rewards and promotions in China are more directly linked to local economic performance, the officials involved do not usually lose sight of the overall performance record, even as they line their own pockets. (3) As elections become more expensive, politicians in India have to be on the lookout for collecting serious money to an extent not necessary in China. But at the same time, there are more institutionalised efforts in India to check the sources of corruption: The Right to Information Act, 2005, for example, which recently came into existence as a result of an energetic public activist movement in India, is an important step in that direction.

The social revolution that democracy has brought about has also had some impact on the nature of governance in India. The diminishing hold of elite control and the welcome expansion of democracy to the lower rungs of the social hierarchy have been associated with a loosening of the earlier administrative protocols and a steady erosion of the institutional insulation of the decision-making process in public administration and economic management. This has affected not just the ability to credibly commit to long-term decisions, but the whole fabric of governance itself. It is now common practice, for example, for a low-caste chief minister in a state to proceed, immediately upon assuming office, to transfer away top civil servants belonging to upper castes and to get pliant bureaucrats from his or her own caste. Some of the new social groups coming to power are even nonchalant in suggesting that all these years, upper classes and castes have looted the state, and now it is their turn. If, in the process, they trample upon some individual rights or some procedural aspects of democratic administration, the institutions that are supposed to kick in to restrain them are relatively weak. Highly corrupt politicians are regularly re-elected by their particular ethnic or local constituencies (which they nurse assiduously even while fleecing the rest of the system). Personal extravagance at state expense by particular ethnic leaders is often a source of community pride for historically disadvantaged groups.

This is part of a fundamental tension between the participatory and procedural aspects of Indian democracy. The unfolding of the logic of populist democracy has itself become a threat to democratic governance. The participatory aspects of democracy and the all-consuming emphasis on electoral mobilisation, often of whole groups (described by journalists as "vote banks"), have led the system to look away from politicians' and their followers' rampant procedural violations, generating a "culture of impunity" that the Indian political system will have to grapple with for quite some time to come. Of course, ultimately, the checks and balances of the ramshackle but still vibrant legal system kick in to curb undue excesses, in a way that is rather rare in China. The independent judiciary, the Election Commission, and a few of the regulatory bodies still function with some degree of insulation from political interference and hold up due process against great odds.

This institutional insulation is much weaker in China, and the "culture of impunity" among top Party officials is more prevalent. But there has been discernible progress in the legal system. As disputes become more complex, political interference, though still substantial, is declining, particularly in matters of commercial law. There is greater transparency than before in the corporate governance of state companies, particularly those listed on overseas stock exchanges. The media and non-governmental organisations, as watchdogs, are more active in India. But corporate ownership of media is a problem for independent investigations in both countries, just in different ways. There is occasional official clamping down on corruption in China (including even summary execution as punishment), but cynical people often describe this as mostly targeted at political enemies or at best small fries, exempting the big fish or cronies of the dominant faction leaders.

The Party has also tentatively started to introduce some form of intraparty democracy at the lower levels, with multiple candidates for positions. It is ironic that Indian democracy, which in the beginning decades allowed for a great deal of intraparty democracy, now has largely deviated from this tradition. In most major national parties, the leaders are often nominated from above. Young and ambitious local politicians, finding their path of upward mobility blocked within the larger parties, often are inclined to go out and form their own parties, thereby acquiring leverage in India's coalition politics. This is one source of the country's increasing political fragmentation, which hinders purposive governance.

I have already discussed the important role that decentralisation of power combined with central control over personnel and promotion plays in Chinese governance. In recent years, the central government has recentralised public finances (as it was facing fiscal erosion by the mid-1990s) and taken on final authority over the personnel and loan decisions of local banks (to check the mounting "nonperforming loans" that local officials indulged in). But even at the county level, local government still has a great deal of power (much more than in India) in privatising state companies, in making regulatory approvals and distributing patronage, in appointing local oversight committees against financial and other irregularities, in appointing and fixing the salaries of judges and public prosecutors, and so on. It is difficult for the central government to control local officials and to wean them away from the cosy rental havens they have built in collusion with local business and commercial interests. In its pursuit of the goals of reducing inequality, stopping land seizures, containing environmental damages, and preventing the frequent regulatory scandals (relating to food and other consumer product safety), the central government faces at least the covert opposition of local officials. Even when the local official is not venal, in an atmosphere of information control, his usual inclination is to suppress bad news, as it may adversely affect his chances of promotion or his reputation.

Yet over more than a quarter century now, the Chinese central leadership has shown a remarkable adaptability to changing circumstances and a capacity to mobilise new support coalitions to protect its political power. Keeping the main focus on economic growth and national glory as the source of its political legitimacy, it has moved away from its earlier constituent groups among peasants and workers, allowing urban–rural disparity to grow and presiding over massive layoffs of workers; it has accommodated the erstwhile "red-hat capitalists" in symbiotic relation with state officials, and gradually co-opted the new private entrepreneurs and professionals (including much of the intelligentsia); through its control of bank lending and regulatory approval of investment, it has skilfully balanced regional and factional interests. It is now trying to move some state resources away from the government-business groups of coastal China (e.g., those connected with what used to be called the "Shanghai coalition"), and has publicly shown a great deal of empathy for hitherto excluded groups in remote rural areas and urban migrants, while still being supportive of markets and general non-interference with thriving private enterprises. By streamlining the rules of succession and establishing clear procedures for term and age limits for leaders, it has restructured the rules of authoritarian hierarchy to increase career predictability and general elite support.

But China is still far from establishing a comprehensive rule-based system and institutionalising a credible set of checks and balances. It has installed a far more decisive and purposive governance structure than India, but its weaker institutional checks (such as the lack of independent judiciary or other regulatory authority) and low capacity for conflict management make it more brittle in the face of a crisis than the messy-looking system in India, for all its flaws. As the economy becomes more complex and social relations become more convoluted and intense, the absence of transparent and accountable processes and the attempts by a "control-freak" leadership to force conformity and lockstep discipline will generate acute tension and informational inefficiency. Several alternative political scenarios for the future in China have been depicted by political speculators, none more plausible than the others; some (wistfully) predict the eventual outbreak of Taiwan or Korea style democracy, but only on a large scale, starting with the big cities; others predict that even if China manages a soft landing into some form of quasi-democracy, it will be of the corrupt oligarchic kind under a predominant party like the one that prevailed in Mexico under the Institutional Revolutionary Party for many decades.

While the Indian system has more institutionalised outlets for letting off steam, it also has more ethnic and religious tensions and centrifugal forces to grapple with. It is appalling governance structure for the delivery of social services, its anomic inability to carry out collective action or to overcome populist hindrances to long-term investment in order to address the infrastructure deficit that is reaching crisis proportions, its over-politicised administration and decision-making processes, and its clogged courts and corrupt police and patronage politics that make a mockery of the rule of law for the common people—all will continue to hobble the process of economic growth and alleviation of its still massive poverty. Yet the differential state capacity and governance performance among different states (better in some South or West Indian states) may generate over time a bit of healthy competition in investment climate and poverty alleviation performance to set examples for the democratic participants in all states to demand, overshadowing the salience of ethnicity or religion in politics.

Both China and India have done much better in the last quarter century than either did in the last 200 years in terms of economic growth. And each country's polity has shown remarkable resilience in its own way. Still, we should not underestimate the structural weaknesses in their governance mechanisms and the enormousness of the social and political uncertainties that cloud the horizons for these two countries.

CHAPTER 2

Poverty and Inequality in China and India Elusive Link with Globalisation

Economic & Political Weekly, 22 September 2007

Most people, I find, have a strong opinion on globalisation, positive or negative. The strength of their opinion is often in inverse proportion to the amount of robust facts they have. The question of how much impact globalisation has had on poverty and inequality in China and India in the last quarter century is an example of this. The pro-globalisers point out that global integration has worked wonders in bringing down the massive poverty that has afflicted these two countries for many decades. Those who are opposed, often point out the large rise in economic inequality that globalisation is supposed to have caused in both countries. In this essay, we suggest that both sides are jumping to conclusions that are not warranted by a closer look at the data.

First, a clarification on the meaning of the term "Globalisation" will be used in this essay. Globalisation means different things to different people. Some interpret it to mean the global reach of new technologies (particularly in information and communication), some refer to the tentacles of corporate capitalism or US hegemony in military, economic and cultural matters. In the context of poverty and inequality in China and India, I shall interpret globalisation in the rather limited sense of openness to foreign trade and (long-term) investment. Over the last two decades, both China and India have made major strides in these aspects of globalisation (China dramatically so, with the merchandise trade ratio to GDP in 2005 exceeding 60 per cent, more than double that for India, and direct foreign investment of $79 billion a year, about 13 times that for India).

CHINESE EXPERIENCE

The standard argument by pro-globalisers has been that the opening up of the economy leads to dynamic benefits, which improve the growth rate, and the latter in turn reduces poverty. The static allocation effect may also be pro-poor as it expands job opportunities for unskilled labour, which is plentiful in poor countries. China has captured the world market in many labour-intensive manufactures, and this has led to a major transformation of the economy, improving the rate of growth and of poverty reduction. It is the case that the rate of growth and the rate of poverty reduction have been nothing short of dramatic in China. Total factor productivity in Chinese industry grew at an annual average of 3.1 per cent in 1978-93 and at double that rate in 1993-04. If one takes the admittedly crude World Bank poverty line of $1 a day per capita (at 1993 purchasing power parity), the proportion of people below that poverty line in China fell from 63.8 per cent in 1981 to 9.9 per cent in 2004. If instead one takes a national poverty line (of 850 Yuan per year for rural China and 1,200 Yuan for urban at 2002 prices), the National Bureau of Statistics data suggest that the poverty proportion declined from 53 per cent to 8 per cent between 1981 and 2001. Never before in history have so many hundreds of millions of people been lifted above the poverty line in such a short period. Since all this happened while the country had a phenomenal opening up of the economy, China has become a poster boy for the international financial press and free-trade economists when they wax eloquent about the poverty-reducing effects of globalisation.

Yet there is no convincing statistical demonstration of this, as no one has yet tested a causal model where, controlling for other factors and applying a suitable identification strategy, global integration has been found to be the main cause of the dramatic decline of poverty in China. In the absence of such a demonstration, a careful eyeballing of the data suggest that the more important reason for the large decline of poverty over the last three decades may actually lie elsewhere. The annual national poverty estimates as well as World Bank estimates referred to above show that the largest part of the decline in poverty already happened by the mid-1980s, before the big strides in foreign trade and investment in China in the 1990s and later. For example, in the former estimates the poverty percentage in 1987 is already about one-third (i.e., 16.8 per cent) that of 1981. In the World Bank estimates, of the half a billion people lifted above the $1 poverty line between 1981 and 2004, about two-thirds got so lifted by 1987.

Much of the extreme poverty was concentrated in rural areas, and its large decline in the first-half of the 1980s is perhaps mainly a result of: (a) the spurt in agricultural growth following de-collectivisation (agricultural output grew at 7.1 per cent per year on an average during 1979-84 compared to 2.7 per cent during 1970-78); (b) land reform, which by an egalitarian redistribution, subject only to differences in regional average and demographic size, provided a floor to rural income; and (c) readjustment of farm procurement prices. These are mostly internal factors that had very little to do with global integration.

Some trade economists have pointed out to me that even in the 1980s, China had a trade expansion in labour-intensive products. There was some expansion in the trade ratio to GDP in the 1980s, and the Special Economic Zone (SEZ) of Shenzen was in operation by the mid-1980s. But in much of the 1980s the most important exports of China were natural resource-intensive products; as late as 1985 the largest single export item was petroleum. (In fact because of dual track pricing it was profitable some years in the 1980s to export petroleum in one price and then to import it in another price!) Since export/import ratios are endogenous, one may look at the decline in (weighted) average tariff rates over the 1980s: the mean tariff rates went down only slightly, from 31.9 per cent in 1980-83 to 29.2 per cent in 1988-90.

In any case, the proportion of the labour force in manufacturing in this period was small, so the large poverty decline in the first-half of the 1980s is unlikely to be attributable to manufacturing exports. It is also worth noting that the poverty percentage, after the sharp drop between 1981 and 1987, went up for much of the period between 1987 and 1994, even as exports of labour-intensive manufactures grew rapidly. This indicates that by 1987 the agricultural spurt has worked itself out and the effect of labour-intensive manufactures was still weak. It was only after the mid-1990s that the poverty percentage started declining again and labour-intensive exports may have played a significant role in it, although even in this period, one should not minimise the effect of (largely) domestic factors like easier migration from rural areas and higher agricultural procurement prices. So without more convincing evidence on the basis of a causal model, I am inclined to believe in the stronger influence of agriculture and land reform in the very large poverty reduction by the mid-1980s.

IN INDIA

In India, the reduction of trade barriers since the 1990s seems to have been associated with an expansion of exports of mostly capital and skill-intensive products (software and business services, pharmaceuticals, vehicles, auto parts, steel, etc), and a more vigorous and competitive corporate sector but most of the economy and workers are outside the corporate sector. A rise in the total factor productivity in industry, from 0.3 per cent in 1978-93 to 1.1 per cent in 1993-2004, has been noted in some estimates. The more significant rise in India is, of course, in the service sector; total factor productivity in that sector grew from an annual average of 1.4 per cent in 1978-93 to 3.9 per cent in 1993-2004. The Indian growth process has been described as service-sector-led growth, whereas in China it has been more manufacturing-centred. One immediately thinks of the widely acclaimed performance of Indian software and other information technology-enabled services. But it seems that in the economy's service sector growth in the period 1993-2004, not all of the growth can be explained by finance, business services or telecommunication where global integration may have made a difference.

A large part of the growth in the service sector, at a rate higher than that in manufacturing, has been in the traditional or "unorganised sector" services, which even in the last decade formed nearly two-thirds of the service sector output. These are provided by tiny enterprises, often below the policy radar, unlikely to have been directly affected substantially by foreign trade policy reforms. It is a matter of some dispute as to how much of the growth in traditional services (mostly non-traded) is explained by the rise in service demand in the rest of the economy (including increased outsourcing by the manufacturing firms, which formerly used to supply those services in-house), and how much is a statistical artefact, as the way the output is measured in these traditional services has been rather shaky all along. So the link between trade reforms and growth in the whole economy is not yet clearly established, even though it is very likely that the general reduction in controls and regulations, and the increased leeway of market discipline and forces of competition (the increase in global market participation is only one part of this process) may have unleashed entrepreneurial energies in both the formal and informal sectors. (I would also like to speculate that the concurrent social changes in India, in the political rise of hitherto subordinate social groups after many centuries of social oppression, may also have played some role in this unleashing of energies.)

Now let us look at the link between growth and poverty reduction in India. Official poverty estimates show that the poverty percentage declined from 44.5 per cent in 1983 to 27.5 per cent in 2004-05. Again the international financial press often attributes this significant (though not dramatic) decline to globalisation. National Sample Survey (NSS) data actually suggest that the rate of decline in poverty has somewhat slowed down in 1993-2005, the period of intensive opening of the economy, compared to the 1970s and 1980s. It may not be unconnected with the fact that agricultural output (and total factor productivity in agriculture) grew at a slower rate in the last decade compared to the earlier decade. This may be largely on account of the decline in public investment in rural infrastructure (like irrigation or prevention of soil erosion), which has little to do with globalisation. We should also recognise that private consumer expenditure data of the NSS that are used in poverty estimates do not capture the declining environmental resources (like forests, fisheries, grazing lands, and water both for drinking and irrigation) on which the daily lives and livelihoods of the poor depend.

There has also been a decline in the rate of growth of real wages in the period 1993-2005 compared to the previous decade 1983-93. As we have already mentioned, India's export expansion in recent years has largely been in capital and skill-intensive industries, unlike in China or Vietnam, and as such may not have helped large numbers of unskilled workers. There is a plethora of opinions on why this has happened in India (some blame restrictive labour laws, some creaking infrastructure, and others the small-scale sector reservation policy for a large number of products, and so on) but a careful statistical study of the significance of these different factors, controlling for other factors, still remains to be done.

Global integration does not seem to have helped some of the non-income indicators like those of health. The National

Family Health Survey (NFHS) data show that some of India's health indicators are worse than those of Bangladesh (in maternal mortality, infant mortality, child immunisation rates, etc), and even those of sub-Saharan Africa (in the percentage of underweight children), in spite of much higher growth rates in India than in those other countries. Percentage of underweight children (below age 3) in India is 46, and about 30 per cent on an average in sub-Saharan Africa (8 per cent in China). Take the case of Gujarat, one of the richest, high growth, and high-reform states in India: the percentage of underweight children, which was already high (higher than sub-Saharan Africa), went up between NFHS 2 (1998-99) and NFHS 3 (2005-06).

Some disaggregated studies across districts in India have also found trade liberalisation slowing down the decline in rural poverty. Such results may indicate the difficulty of displaced farmers and workers in adjusting to new activities and sectors on account of various constraints (for example, in getting credit or information or infrastructural facilities like power and roads, large incidence of school dropouts, and labour market rigidities), even when new opportunities are opened up by globalisation. This is in line with textbooks in international economics where it is emphasised that product market liberalisation need not be an improvement when there are severe distortions in input markets. In terms of policy, this calls for complementary policies (in credit, labour markets, and in social and economic infrastructure) to mitigate the possible adverse effects of trade liberalisation on some poor people.

The Indian pace of poverty reduction has been less than China's, not just because growth has been faster in China but also because the same 1 per cent growth rate reduces (or is associated with reduction in) poverty in India by much less. The so-called growth elasticity of poverty reduction is much higher in China than India; this may have something to do with the differential inequalities in wealth in the two countries (particularly, land and education). Contrary to common perception, these inequalities are much higher in India than in China. The Gini coefficient of land distribution in rural India was 0.74 in 2003; the corresponding figure in China was 0.49 in 2002. India's educational inequality is one of the worst in the world: according to a table in the *World Development Report 2006*, published by the World Bank, the Gini coefficient of the distribution of adult schooling years in the population, a crude measure of educational inequality, was 0.56 in India in 1998-2000, which is not just higher than 0.37 in China in 2000 but even higher than almost all Latin American countries (Brazil: 0.39).

Comparing across states in India, the estimated growth elasticity of poverty reduction depends on initial distribution of land and human capital. In the period 1977-2001, this elasticity was quite low in high growth states like Maharashtra and Karnataka, and high in states like Kerala and West Bengal. Similarly, comparing across states in China, growth had more poverty-reducing impact in initially less unequal provinces.

GLOBALISATION AND INEQUALITY

The link between globalisation and inequality is also not very clear. Theoretically, globalisation may open opportunities for some people (not all of whom are rich), and may cause hardships for those whose livelihoods are ruined by competition. (The analogy with the mighty rivers that flow into the deltas of India, creating new fertile land on one bank, and destroying land, habitations and livelihoods on the other, comes to mind.) Much depends on how society and the political community compensates and rehabilitates the displaced. On the latter, the recent history in both China and India has been rather dismal in general.

While international trade theory points to the potential of gainers compensating the losers and still keeping some gains from trade, the politics of redistribution are much more messy and depends on the social and political institutions of a country. At the same time one should emphasise that the obstacles to (and vested interests against) redistributive policies are often mainly domestic in origin (particularly for large countries like China or India). Closing the economy does not reduce the power of the relevant vested interests. It is also the case that international trade theory is often preoccupied with costs of production, while a large part of success in exports depends on marketing and distribution, which often require large initial investment, managerial skills and development of networks. The international retail chains that provide the latter often charge monopoly margins absorbing much of the gains of trade liberalisation, and very little may trickle down to the poor producers in small farms and firms.

Empirically, there are very few reliable studies for China or India that test a causal model linking globalisation with inequality at the appropriate disaggregate level. At least two major problems beset the empirical analyst in this matter. One is that so many other changes have taken place in the last quarter century in these two countries, it is difficult to disentangle the effect of globalisation from that of other on-going changes (like technological progress—often skill-biased—demographic changes or regulatory and macroeconomic policies). Secondly, in both countries there are reasons to suspect that economic inequality (or its rise) is underestimated because of a widely-noted fact facing household surveys (in many countries) of large (and increasing) non-response by rich households. It is also difficult to compare China and India, as most of the inequality data that are cited in this context usually are for income inequality for China and consumption expenditure inequality for India (as the NSS does not collect income data). The latter two disparate sources do show a rise in expenditure inequality in both countries in the last decade or so. But, as we have suggested, this rise may be an underestimate, and there is very little analysis as yet to show that this rise is primarily due to globalisation.

Even if global integration were to be causally linked with higher growth, the link between growth and inequality is not always clear. In China, the periods of rapid growth did not necessarily bring more rapid increases in income inequality; the periods of falling inequality (1981-85 and 1995-98) had among the highest growth rates in average household income. In China, provinces with more global exposure and higher growth did not have larger rise in inequality. With the Gini coefficient of income in coastal China went up from 0.35 in 1991 to 0.39 in 2000, the corresponding rise in the interior provinces was from 0.39 to 0.48. In the coastal provinces, a more rapid job growth in the non-state sector helped reduce the urban-rural income differential there. In India, the relative income divergence between states is increasing (more than in China) but it is hard to separate the effects of globalisation from those of differential conditions of infrastructure and business-friendly policies in different states.

In both countries, periods of high agricultural growth may have reduced overall inequality, and the recent decline in agricultural growth rates may have had some influence in the rising inequality. For the urban sector in both countries, there is some evidence of a faster rate of rise in the wage rate for those with higher education. According to the estimates by the Asian Development Bank, the Gini coefficient of average real wages of urban full-time employees in India went up from 0.38 in 1983 to 0.47 in 2004. This increase in wage inequality is consistent with the skill-intensity of Indian economic growth (that the trade reforms may have played some role in) and the looming talent shortage that the corporate sector is complaining about. In urban China also, the rate of return to college (and above) education compared to, say, high school education has more than doubled since the early 1990s. In both China and India, it is again difficult to separate the effect of the on-going skill-biased technological progress from that of globalisation. But compared to China, the backwardness of India in the education sector (for example, even among new entrants in the labour force, among the 15-24 age-group nearly a quarter in India are illiterate, almost none in China) and in the status of women (for example, female labour force participation in urban China is above 70 per cent, only 24 per cent in urban India) imply that the forces that perpetuate wage inequality are stronger in India, and these forces are largely domestic in origin.

The contentious debates on globalisation in the media as well as in academia often lead to a volley of sweeping and unthinking generalisations, in particular about China and India, the two awakening giants in the global economy. It is time for a great deal of caution and reasoned and rigorous empirical analysis before we pronounce judgments on the effects of globalisation on poverty and inequality in these two countries.

CHAPTER 3

Challenges for China at Sixty

YaleGlobal, 25 September 2009

As the sixtieth anniversary of the People's Republic of China approaches (the sixtieth anniversary of the founding of the People's Republic of China took place on 1 October 2009.), one is prone to reflect generally on its dramatic recent history, including the historic irony of the development of today's arguably most vigorous capitalism in an avowedly communist country. The contradictions involved here are much more than what were dreamt of in Mao's philosophy when he famously speculated on the nature of contradictions, first in a 1937 essay, where he stated: "The law of contradiction in things, that is, the law of the unity of opposites, is the fundamental law of nature and of society."

While the Party retains the monopoly of power, the market mechanism is the major allocator of resources in the Chinese economy—much like it was in Taiwan during the authoritarian days of KMT, an anti-communist party organised on quasi-Leninist lines. Most people would agree that the private sector is now the more dynamic part of the Chinese economy and creates most of the jobs; in order to find out how much of the (non-farm) economy is actually under private ownership is not straightforward: it is not easy to classify Chinese firms by their ownership or to distinguish between private and public or semi-public control rights. Even in China's most famous private companies, Lenovo and Huawei Technologies, the ownership structure is quite convoluted, as Yasheng Huang indicates in his book, *Capitalism with Chinese Characteristics.* This is, of course, part of the legacy of the development of the Chinese private sector under the shadow of the Party-controlled state. As late as 1988, private firms with more than 8 employees were not permitted. Many private firms operated below the radar and used various subterfuges and covert deals with local officials, as they adapted themselves to the changing permissible mores. Some of them used to be called "red-hat capitalists", sometimes hiding under the façade of local collectives. Only since the late 90's did they slowly take off their red hats and start coming out of the closet. Many of the smaller and regional State-owned Enterprises (SOEs) were privatised and often their managers became the new owners. Today, probably more than half of the non-farm output (though not of fixed capital investment) is primarily privately owned or controlled. Currently about one-third of the private entrepreneurs are members of the Party (including "xiahai" entrepreneurs who are former officials); membership helps them get state finance, and more protection and legitimacy.

Of course, it is well-known that some of the entrepreneurs are in fact friends or relatives of Party officials. (An article in *Der Spiegel*, 27 February 2007, reported a finding by the Chinese Academy of Social Sciences and the Party's Central University that of the 3,320 Chinese citizens with a personal wealth of 100 million Yuan or about $14 million, 2,932 were children of high-ranking Party officials.) Many SOEs are also controlled by powerful political families. Thus there is a new political-managerial class, which over the last two decades has converted their positions of authority into wealth and power. The vibrancy of entrepreneurial ambitions combined with the arbitrariness of power in an authoritarian state has sometimes given rise to particularly corrupt or predatory forms of capitalism, unencumbered by the restraints of civil society institutions. Perhaps nowhere has the predation been as starkly evident as in land seizures both in cities and the countryside. In the real estate boom of recent years, for example, the commercial developers in cahoots with local officials have bulldozed old city neighbourhoods, residents waking up in the morning to find that their house has been marked for demolition with the Chinese character "chai"— meaning raze—painted in white, with hardly any redress or adequate compensation available.

This corrupt or predatory form of capitalism has also some obvious global implications. When foreign companies try to invest in China or Chinese companies try to acquire holdings abroad the decision-making process can be vitiated by arbitrary political interference, underhand dealings, kickbacks and influence-peddling. Even in matters of foreign aid in Africa a recent *The New York Times* report points to the opacity in the activities of politically well-connected Chinese foreign-aid contractors.

While the state has relaxed its earlier control over prices and allows markets and profit-making to be the major organising principle of domestic economic life, it is still predominant in the capital goods sectors and in transportation and finance. Some of the SOEs are now important players in the global market competition. In general, in recruiting professional managers, broadening their investor base, and shedding their traditional social and political obligations, many SOEs do not conform to the usual stereotypes about SOEs. The state still controls the larger and often more profitable (high-margin, monopolistic) companies in the industrial and service sectors. The state's role in regulating the private sector also goes far beyond the usual functions in other countries. Apart from exerting indirect control rights in private firms, during the current global recession some SOEs, flush with abundant loans from state banks, have even taken over some of the

financially-strapped   small   and   medium-size   private
enterprises. As a senior Chinese banker commented (quoted
in the *Financial Times*, 24 August 2009), "It's quite hard to
compete when you are playing against the referee."
An important question arises in cases where an enterprise
is managed on essentially commercial principles, but the state
still has control rights over a large share of the assets: is this
a capitalist enterprise? Some may describe it as capitalist if the
principle of shareholder value maximisation is followed
(though this principle is not always followed in capitalist
countries—say, in Japan or Germany). Others may point out
that as long as substantial control rights remain with the state,
which is subject to ever-malleable and potentially arbitrary
political considerations, the internal dynamic logic of
capitalism is missing, and politics take command. In late 2008,
when China's richest man, Huang Guangyu was arrested,
many thought that his biggest crime was that he was getting
too powerful for the leaders' comfort (shades of Putin's
Russia).
Nevertheless, it is probably reasonable to guess (though
it may not be enough to reassure the global business
community) that while the Party can undo individual
capitalists at short notice, it will be much more difficult for
the leadership to unravel a whole network of capitalist
relations, by now thickly overlaid with various vested
interests knotted with "guanxi" ties. Individual entrepreneurs
have a clientelistic relationship with the state, but the state,
for all its relative autonomy, is now sufficiently enmeshed
in a profit-oriented system that has been identified with
legitimacy-enhancing international economic prowess and
nationalist glory, a tiger that the political leadership may find
difficult to dismount. At the local level, the central
leadership, even while holding the important instrument of
career promotion for local officials, often finds it difficult to
rein them in as they collude with local business to commit
some of the worst capitalist excesses (in land acquisitions,

product safety violations or toxic pollution). In any case, by an official account, the Communist Party composition itself has drastically changed; the majority of members now are no longer workers or peasants, but professionals, college students and businessmen.

Such are the ambiguities and contradictions of Chinese capitalism that Comrade Mao never foresaw, nor did the capitalist corporations in the West now dealing with this strange hybrid.

CHAPTER 4

The State of Health Services in China and India in a Larger Context

Health Affairs, July/August 2008

China and India have had a remarkable period of economic growth over the last quarter century, and as a result there has been a significant decline in mass poverty in these two large poor countries, more dramatically so in China. But this impressive economic growth and decline of income poverty have not been adequately reflected in some general features in the lives of the poor, particularly in the crucial matter of health. There are some egregious 'failures' of both market and government in the sphere of health services in all countries, but they have been particularly acute in China and India. We shall discuss this problem in the larger context of the political and economic structure in the two countries, and show that the structural deficiencies from which the problem arises are similar as well as different in the two cases.

In some broad aggregative measures of health outcome, the Chinese performance has been much better than India's, and it has been so for several decades. For example, life expectation at birth now in India is what it used to be in China in the early 70's; in infant mortality by 1975 China achieved a rate which India did not reach even in 2000. To this we may add that of

India's under-three children as many as 46 per cent are underweight, compared to China's 8 per cent. Under-five child mortality rate in India is more than twice that of China. There are, of course, some differences in initial conditions between the two countries. India being in general nearer the tropics than most of China, one expects a larger incidence of certain diseases in India, and conditions of vector control may be more difficult, other things remaining the same. According to WHO estimates for 1998, the burden of infectious and parasitic diseases (measured in terms of DALY's—disability-adjusted life years—per capita) is 7 times as high in India compared to China. This may be partly the result of differences in physical and climatic conditions. But only partly, as this is also partly an outcome of relative policy deficiency. Socialist China had a much more vigorous policy of public health and sanitation than India, and also a larger army of paramedics pressed into basic public health service in the villages. By the middle 70's, China had a rudimentary system of medical insurance (called "cooperative health services") that covered the overwhelming majority of rural people, something that did not exist in India. Also, the Chinese government showed an ability to mobilise campaigns for preventive health care and against public health threats that were impressive by most developing country standards.

In contrast, India after Independence never had any system of public health and sanitation anywhere on that scale. There has been no systematic planning and delivery of public health services (as opposed to curative medical services) or sustained large-scale disease control. As M Dasgupta has pointed out in a 2005 World Bank Policy Research Paper, in India "there is strong capacity for dealing with (disease) outbreaks when they occur, but not to prevent them from occurring. Impressive capacity also exists for conducting intensive campaigns, but not for sustaining these gains on a continuing basis after the campaign. This is illustrated by the near-eradication of malaria through highly-organised efforts in the 1950s, and its resurgence when attention shifted to other priorities such as family planning". This situation about public health and preventive care is not entirely unconnected with the political-economy factors being quite different in India compared to China in the early socialist decades. With the advance of antibiotics the elite in India felt less threatened than in the past by the spread of communicable diseases among the poor, leading to a policy de-emphasis on environmental hygiene, and they succeeded in diverting public funds to high-end curative treatment in big urban hospitals, away from rudimentary but effective and widespread health services in the villages of the kind China used to have.

In the last quarter century of economic reform, there has been a sea-change in public health policy in China. With de-collectivisation of 1978-79, the rural health services collapsed. The paramedics who used to be paid in work points at the production brigade and team levels now lacked a systematic method of compensation. Soon the total number of paramedics became less than a quarter of what it used to be in the 70's. By mid-1980's the "cooperative health services" covered less than 10 per cent of the rural population (and the latter mostly lingering in the better-off coastal areas). In general, with the collapse of local public finances, particularly in remote rural areas, fewer resources were devoted to public health. There was a decline even in curative services; the total number of hospital beds per thousand rural residents in 2003 was about half of what it was 20 years back. Yet these 20 years saw phenomenal economic growth in China. While the basic indicators of public health kept on improving, the pace was slower than before, and worked particularly badly for rural girls. For example, between 1981 and 2000, while infant mortality for boys went down from 40 per thousand to 25.8, that for girls went down much slower, from 38.1 to 36.7.

China essentially moved in this period from one of the most impressive basic public health coverage systems to a largely privatised (or privately financed) system, particularly in rural areas. In the cities, formal sector employees have some form of health insurance, but there too over time premiums and fees paid by patients increased considerably. The poor had to bear the brunt, as even in the cities most of them are in the uncovered part of the population, migrants and informal sector workers. Yip and Mahal in a 2008 paper in *Health Affairs* point out that 76 per cent of the lowest-income quintile urban individuals do not have health insurance; the corresponding percentage in the lowest-income quintile rural individuals is 80 per cent. This has implied that many sick people do not seek medical care, largely on account of financial hardship; Yip and Mahal cite data that in 2003 nearly half of those reporting an illness did not seek outpatient care. Those who do, spend an inordinate proportion of their income on health care; according to their data, the poorest quintile individuals in rural areas spend as much as 27 per cent of their income on health care, and in the poorest urban quintile it is 11 per cent.

This large change in the public funding basis of health services in China is linked with a systemic problem relating to decentralised development. China is often cited as a glowing example of industrialisation under decentralisation. Regional economic decentralisation provided autonomy and incentives, and in the 1980's and 1990's local industries flourished under the control of local governments and collectives. The so-called township and village enterprises (now largely privatised over the last decade) provided leadership to the phenomenal industrial growth in China over the last quarter century. Beyond a minimum amount of taxes for the higher-level governments, the local governments were allowed to keep the residual surplus, with all the positive incentive thus provided for encouraging local enterprise and making money. There was also the pressure that failing enterprises will not in general be bailed out by higher-level governments. This combination of incentives and pressure worked in many localities, particularly those with better connections for market and finance. But one side effect of economic decentralisation is acute regional inequality. Coastal China surged ahead, and local governments there flush with profits from the enterprises under their control could buttress the social services, as their funding source from the communes disintegrated all over the country. But the interior or agriculture-dominant provinces and remote areas, where these enterprises were few and profitable ones fewer, were largely left to their own devices when it came to funding social services. Then the fiscal reforms of 1994 centralised revenue collection and allocation, and many local areas were left with unfunded mandates for basic social services including health. The fiscal reforms of more recent years clamped down on some of the arbitrary fees and taxes that many local governments had imposed on the local population, leaving them more financially strapped. An indicator of increasing regional disparity in provision of health care can be gauged from the fact that in 1985 the total number of technical medical personnel per thousand people was somewhat lower in city than in county; 20 years later, it was more than twice in city than in county. It is also no coincidence that, as Yip and Mahal estimate, the crude measures of inter-provincial inequality (such as the coefficient of variation) in aggregative health outcomes like life expectancy at birth or infant mortality increased in 20 years since 1980.

While China moved away from an egalitarian and impressive basic health service of the socialist period, India has remained dismal and in-egalitarian all through. Only about 15 per cent of the people in India have any health insurance (primarily through their employers), and the share of out of pocket spending in total health spending exceeds 70 per cent, which is higher than in China (though it has increased faster in the latter country). Appearances to the contrary, health care in India is predominantly private (which is largely unregulated). Household survey data suggest that 85 per cent of all visits for health care in rural areas, even by the poorest people, are to private practitioners. While the poor quality of service in public clinics and hospitals (and absenteeism by nurses and doctors) often drive patients to private doctors (some of them quacks or crooks) in India, in China the high fees charged in public health clinics (and the latters' concentration on revenue-generating activities) in effect turn them into for-profit private providers. As Yip and Mahal point out, in India unlike China at least the public facilities receive the bulk of their revenues from government subsidies and they provide their (often paltry and poor-quality) services at low cost to those who are too poor to afford the more expensive private care (although rampant corruption renders the public service provided not entirely free).

In both countries, doctors often over-medicate and refer patients to unnecessary diagnostic tests, driving up health costs in general. This is part of a general market failure in health care, where the decider (the doctor) is not the purchaser (the patient). In poor countries, with little information and education, the problem is exacerbated as the patients themselves sometimes show preference for unnecessary antibiotics and steroids, which the quacks oblige them with. In both countries, the more important problem is a governance failure. The public health delivery system is afflicted by poor provider incentives, coupled with low accountability to the patients.

First of all, the medical personnel are paid a fixed salary independent of the number of patients or of their visits, so they have no economic incentive to serve them. In China, some of their non-fixed salary is in terms of commissions on drug sales, with effects on over-prescription. Secondly, there is little monitoring or punishment for laxity in service. Thirdly, the poor have very little organised 'voice' in sanctioning the errant provider. In the otherwise vibrant democracy of India, in most areas the state of local democracy is not strong enough to keep public service providers accountable to the local citizens.

Periodic elections provide a rather blunt instrument for keeping public officials in check, and in any case the electoral agenda are full of multiplicity of pressing issues of which poor health service is only one among many. Besides, politicians find it easier to claim credit for inaugurating a big hospital or installing new equipment there than for regular maintenance of services or public sanitation and vector control. In China, the channels of local accountability are even weaker. In both countries, local social groups and NGOs provide some accountability pressure in localised pockets.

In both countries, there is now a renewed effort on part of the government to press more resources into and improve the delivery of public health services. The Chinese programme seems more ambitious, in attempting to provide a partially subsidised universal basic health care, and they have more budgetary resources to devote to this. But in both countries, the governance and accountability issues mentioned earlier will not be resolved easily. In India, the weakness of local democracy coupled with a corrupt and inert bureaucracy dissipate many a well-intentioned policy measure from above. In China, how effective and adequate the actual implementation of the ambitious programme will be remains to be seen. Over the last several years the constant chanting of the 'harmonious society' mantra by the central leadership has not always succeeded in reining in local officials from their hitherto single-minded, frantic (and lucrative) pursuit of income growth often at the expense of social welfare. Besides, the fundamental problem of equity and quality of social services remains when both the bureaucracy and the provider are bound to act according to their self-interest if their incentive system is not restructured, and when the intended beneficiaries are not well-informed about what is best for them and often lack the 'voice' or power to sanction even when they are.

CHAPTER 5

The Slowing of Two Economic Giants

The New York Times, 14 July 2013

The world's two most populous countries are slowing down.
To be sure, China's output is expected to grow by 7.8 per cent
this year, and India's by 5.6 per cent—far superior to
2 per cent for Japan, 1.7 per cent for the United States,
0.9 per cent for Britain and shrinkage (*negative* 0.6 per cent) in
the troubled euro zone, the International Monetary Fund
projected last week.

But there is no sequel in sight for the 10-per cent-plus
growth China and India posted in 2010. The West can no
longer count on their continued expansion to lift its sagging
economies. For 2.5 billion people, the consequences are more
dire: in India, less money to strengthen the threadbare social
safety net, and in China, possible political instability. What
does the slowdown mean for these two giants, and which will
come out ahead?

Let us start with China, the bigger of the two economies.
Talk of a global "Beijing consensus"—state-controlled
capitalism as an alternative to the "Washington consensus"
about how poor countries should develop—has largely
disappeared. China's new leaders are focused on problems at
home: battling corruption, reining in the overheated housing

market, scaling back the government's outsize role in the economy, and cracking down on financial speculation. China may be close to exhausting the possibilities of technological catch-up with the West, particularly in manufacturing. For China to move up the value chain, and become an advanced-manufacturing powerhouse like Germany, it must move beyond off-the-shelf technology and copying rival designs and reap gains from genuine innovation, which can come about only through research and development.

China has amassed huge foreign exchange reserves, partly by keeping the value of its currency low. It now has to rebalance its economy away from the construction boom and financial speculation and toward private consumption and improvements in pensions, health care and other forms of social protection. Crony capitalism has been allowed to misallocate capital toward too-big-to-fail, low-productivity state-owned firms operated by loyal apparatchiks and away from dynamic private small firms.

Concentrated wealth poses problems for both countries. The Hurun Report, a Shanghai-based wealth monitor, estimated last year that the 83 richest delegates to the National People's Congress and an advisory group, the Chinese People's Political Consultative Conference, had a net worth of over $250 billion. By comparison, the declared assets of all of the roughly 545 members of the Lok Sabha, the lower house of India's Parliament, amount to only about $2 billion.

In India, the collusion between Indian billionaires and politicians, while rampant, is somewhat less direct and more subject to political and media scrutiny. In China, collusion between Party officials and commercial interests, especially at the local level, has caused widespread popular anger against arbitrary land acquisition and toxic pollution.

The economist and philosopher Amartya Sen recently argued that India has lagged behind China because it had not invested enough in education and health care, which raise living standards and labour productivity. He rightly emphasises that deficient social services and the inequality that results are not just a matter of social justice, but of economic growth as well, as the history of much of East Asia shows. But one should not get the impression that progress in social services is by itself sufficient for growth. Exemplary welfare programmes in the state of Kerala in India, and in Sri Lanka, have not been matched by spectacular economic performance. The latter also requires improvements in infrastructure, less cumbersome regulations and a culture that fosters entrepreneurial investment.

Professor Sen raises but does not examine a puzzle: why voters in the world's largest democracy cannot get politicians to effectively deliver social services. Infant and maternal mortality and poor sanitation are not salient electoral issues. This is partly because India's fractious society (more heterogeneous than China's) has often emphasised uplifting the dignity of former oppressed social groups over basic good governance.

What of the Chinese model? The history of developing countries shows that authoritarianism is neither necessary nor sufficient for development. The Communist Party will find it increasingly tough to manage a complicated economy (without independent regulators) and political system (without an independent judiciary or effective rule of law).

Without innovation, China cannot sustain high growth, as the artificially low prices of land and capital for politically favoured firms become difficult to maintain and the supply of cheap labour dwindles. Unlike in India, a significant slowdown could be regime-threatening for China—today's young people, with higher expectations than their forebears, will have less tolerance for a shortage of good jobs and affordable housing. China's leaders may be riding a tiger that will be hard to dismount.

On the other hand, India's experience, like America's, shows how partisan fragmentation in a rambunctious democracy can undermine effective governance. In the last few years the headline economic stories in India have been about pervasive corruption: politicised allocation of high-value public resources (land, mineral rights, oil and gas, telecommunications), shady public-private partnerships and the galloping cost of elections financed by the illicit incomes of politicians. India's administrative system, where promotion has little connection to performance, encourages even more malfeasance than China's. But India has independent judges, government auditors and a free press—checks on corruption that are absent in China.

CHAPTER 6

Taking a Wrong Turn

Hindustan Times, 26 October 2010

The stories of mismanagement before the start of the recently-completed (3-14 October 2010) Commonwealth Games in New Delhi and of the hysterical reaction in Beijing to the announcement of the Nobel Peace Prize award to Liu Xiaobo illustrate in their different ways the complexity of national political culture in India and China now strutting in a global playing field and the self-image of their elite.

In the build-up to the Commonwealth Games, a relatively minor international sporting event, the scandals of ineptitude and corruption around the construction projects became a matter of widespread scathing commentary in the Indian media. The Indian urban elite, which are itching to bask in the glory of their country's much-awaited climbing the global ranks of big powers, often described this as a matter of national humiliation; the comparison with the superb Chinese organisation of the much bigger Olympics event merely two years back was found particularly galling. For these elite, it is not quite a matter of national humiliation that India continues to be the world's largest country of illiterates and school dropouts, of child and maternal mortality, of stunted and underweight children. In broad health and education indicators, India today is where

China was 40 years back, long before economic reform and high growth started there. Even in India's economically most-advanced state, Gujarat, the proportion of malnourished children is much larger than in sub-Saharan Africa.

The scathing commentary in the Indian media around the 2010 Commonwealth Games also reminds one about the sharp contrast with a major suppressed scandal in China around the time of the Beijing Olympics. A few weeks before the 2008 Olympics, there was what came to be called later the tainted milk scandal in China. The scandal caused outrage among consumers and fraught parents and led to an international outcry about the standards of food safety in China. Nearly three hundred thousand children fell sick and many perished. Yet, before it happened, scribes who knew about the tainted milk were officially asked to suppress the news in view of the imminent Olympics, which was being stage-managed as China's moment of international glory. Somehow most of the Chinese elite, who were basking in superpower glory, did not consider this tragedy a matter of national humiliation.

Chinese official agencies have now declared the award of the Nobel Peace Prize to the jailed human rights activist Liu Xiaobo, as an affront against Chinese national dignity and a malicious attempt to impose Western values on Chinese society. (One indignant Chinese 'netizen' announced that from now on he would avoid Norwegian salmon, another vowed that next time he goes to Macao for gambling, he will boycott Norwegian prostitutes.) The officials, of course, blithely ignore that China is a signatory to the United Nations Declaration on Human Rights, and freedom of expression and protest is ornamentally a part of Article 35 of the Chinese Constitution. These 'Western' values of non-violent dissent are vociferously practised in several non-Western countries, including India where some have even traced these values to ancient Indian political philosophy and practice.

What is worrying is that this is not just Chinese official over-reaction and propaganda. Last year a prominent Beijing intellectual told me that dissidents like Liu Xiaobo have marginalised themselves in the Chinese intellectual community by aligning their cause too much to the West. This kind of attitude even among visionaries makes it easy for the Chinese leadership to portray any external criticism of the regime as a slur on Chinese self-respect and any dissent as sedition. In both China and India, particularly among the middle classes, a kind of preening nationalism is raging. Of course, Indian political culture has been somewhat more tolerant of dissent and diversity, and electoral arithmetic often makes compromise and co-optation of dissenting groups necessary. Yet much of the rest of the country looks away—or regards it as the necessary price for keeping the nation state intact—as gross abuse of human rights and violence by the Indian Army and paramilitary regularly take place in Kashmir, Manipur and Bastar (Chhattisgarh) often reciprocated by the rebels. In different parts of India, the Hindu nationalist forces raise their ugly head, politically and socially, and win elections from time to time.

In the nationalist paranoia about Western values one often forgets that the ideology of the nation state with its homogenising and aggrandising propensities is itself an import from the West. Western history is littered with the devastation at home and abroad caused by the overbearing Nation State. The memory of colonial oppression and defeat by the West and the longstanding reality of its international economic and military domination add fuel to the ultra-nationalism in Asia, both on the chauvinist right and the anti-imperialist left. The misdeeds and the ambiguity of a country's own history do not deter the nationalist zeal and myth-making. As the 19th century French philosopher, Ernst Renan, famously said, part of being a nation is to get its history wrong. About 100 years ago, at a time when a fervent nationalist movement in India was surging all around, Rabindranath Tagore wrote novels and essays that pointedly showed how harmful nationalism can be—"with all its paraphernalia of power and prosperity, its flags and pious hymns".

CHAPTER 7

On Asian Ultra-Nationalism

YaleGlobal, 28 April 2008

As the troubled Olympic torch relay winds its way to Beijing, the recent fury in China about the evil doings of the "Dalai clique" in Tibet and of the Western media goes beyond the ever-active orchestration by the Chinese leadership. As nationalism has replaced socialism as the social glue in this vast country, old memories of humiliation at foreign hands and current pride in phenomenal economic success generate popular resentment at what looks like external attempts to rain on the parade of China's glorious Olympic moment.

Of course, the Chinese protestation that the West is politicising a sports event is disingenuous, as all parties concerned, including the Chinese government, treat it as much more than a sports event. The government now tries to tame the anti-West passions of the people and has made some gestures, at best half-hearted and likely futile, toward negotiation with the Tibetans. Modulating the mass passions and keeping them under appropriate bounds so that they do not boomerang back is a tough job, as Chinese administrators know very well. But serious Chinese social thinkers cannot be comfortable about the preening nationalism all around them, often stoked by the frenzy of the internet mob—witness the harassment and persecution of a Chinese student at Duke

University and her family in China on grounds that she committed the grievous offense of trying to mediate between two opposed groups of demonstrators on the occasion of the campus protests around Tibet. Nor can the Chinese thinkers be unaware, that despite tight state control over sources of information, the economic, political, cultural domination—and migration of the Han Chinese will keep on fuelling unrest in Tibet even when the current opportunist protests die down.

Nationalism in all countries whirls around the great tradition and rides roughshod over the "little people" and their distinctiveness. China in particular has a long history of homogenisation of culture and language, and suppression of voices of dissent, reflexively taken as signs of rebellion. The historian W J F Jenner in his book "The Tyranny of History", describes one of the basic tenets of Chinese civilisation as "that uniformity is inherently desirable, that there should be only one empire, one culture, one script, one tradition". Even feeble movements for autonomy among the Tibetans and Uighurs are thus treated as sedition or "splittist". This way the moderates in these movements are discredited, often radicalising the leadership in the long run and providing the ingredients of self-fulfilling prophecy of the ruling authority in their efforts at suppression.

The composite fabric of Indian civilisation has been woven with different shades of textures and colours. No exaggeration to say that since ancient times India has been a melting-pot of races and cultures. Notwithstanding regular Army incursions in Kashmir, turmoil in North-East, Hindu nationalist forces raising their ugly head politically and socially, winning elections too, sometimes, the Indian political culture has been rather tolerant of pluralism.

They regularly question the national loyalty of other religious groups and justify atrocities on them. Even sporting events become political when, during an India-Pakistan cricket match, the Hindu fanatics look for traitorous signs of jubilation among Indian Muslim spectators if the Pakistan team scores.

Majoritarian violence against ethnic minorities is also familiar in the recent history of Malaysia and Indonesia. Xenophobia has been almost a state-propagated religion in North Korea and Myanmar. In all these countries, the minorities are routinely branded as anti-national. And earlier in the first few decades of the 20th century, militant nationalism that grew in strength in Japan wreaked havoc in much of Asia.

As has been stated before in the preceding chapter, in many of these countries the ideology of the nation state with its homogenising and aggrandising propensities was an import from the West. Western history is littered with the devastation at home and abroad caused by the overbearing nation state. The memory of colonial oppression and defeat by the West and the longstanding reality of its international economic and military domination add fuel to the ultra-nationalism in Asia, both on the chauvinist right and the anti-imperialist left. The misdeeds and the ambiguity of a country's own history do not deter the nationalist zeal and myth-making. As the 19th-century French philosopher, Ernst Renan, famously said, part of being a nation is to get its history wrong.

Surely, nationalism is not without its benefits, especially in countries where divisive conflicts among different parochial communities tear society apart. Particularly in socially extreme heterogeneous countries like India or Indonesia, nationalism can play a role in taming and transcending the internecine-group conflicts and chaos. But while there may be occasions when one wants to give some primacy to the national identity over other cultural or regional identities, this should not be an argument for suppressing the latter or letting the national identity supersede the larger values of humanitarianism.

India is somewhat fortunate in having Gandhi, Nehru and Tagore as intellectual mentors in the independence movement against the coloniser, as all three warned against the excesses of nationalism. Gandhi called imperialism another name of armed nationalism, which he regarded as a curse.

In particular, Tagore, one of India's greatest writers and thinkers, was most trenchant in his criticism of nationalism—even though two of his songs became, posthumously, the national anthems of India and of Bangladesh. About a hundred years back, as has been mentioned earlier, even at a time when a fervent nationalist movement in India was surging all around, he wrote novels and essays that pointedly showed how harmful nationalism can be—"with all its paraphernalia of power and prosperity, its flags and pious hymns"—how in the name of national unity the majority often tramples on minority concerns and aspirations for self-expression, and how national conceit makes society lose its moral balance.

Exactly hundred years back, in 1908, Tagore wrote in a letter to a friend: "Patriotism cannot be our final spiritual shelter; my refuge is humanity. I will not buy glass for the price of diamonds, and I will never allow patriotism to triumph over humanity as long as I live." During an invited lecture on Nationalism in Japan in 1916, Tagore praised Japan for its impressive national achievements and for inspiring self-confidence among other Asian people, but he was open in his sharp criticism on the rise of militant nationalism there. The Japanese public, earlier effusive about him, considerably cooled its reception in subsequent days. In 1938, shortly after the Japanese invasion of China, when a Japanese poet and friend wrote to Tagore, seeking moral support of Japan's action since China was being "saved" from the clutches of the West, Tagore was severely critical and described the Japanese poet's sentiments as translating "military swagger into spiritual bravado".

At a time when Asian countries are becoming more important economically and geo-politically, they should be wary of the dangers of ultra-nationalism and the damages it can cause to their own society and to others, as the history of nation states in the West illustrates so tragically.

VII

INDIAN POLITY AND ECONOMY

CHAPTER 1

Why is Reform Unpopular?

YaleGlobal, 3 October 2006

Despite the hype in the international media about India's global integration, economic reform in India has been halting and hesitant. Many cheerleaders of reform among corporate tycoons and financial columnists are unaware how unpopular reform is, rightly or wrongly, among the general public in India. In the National Election Survey 2004, more than two thirds of about 23,000 sample respondents who had any opinion on the subject say that the reforms benefit only the rich or none at all. Politicians are, of course, too savvy not to notice this. Even the ruling parties over the last decade that supported reforms played them down during election time. Any party that initiates some reforms is quick to oppose them once out of power.

This duplicity is currently on display within the left: In the states where they hold power, they are often driven by the inexorable logic of fiscal near-bankruptcy and competition for investment to be pro-reform; but in Delhi their leaders regularly indulge in ideological grandstanding. Opposition is not confined to the left. The recent reversal of a cabinet decision toward some privatisation was under pressure from a non-left regional party. Trade unions of the right as well as left parties are opposed to privatisation and labour reform. The Gandhians are vocal against the lifting of the policy of reservation, which currently limits more than 500 products— from bicycle parts to electronic equipment—exclusively for the small-scale industries. In the National Election Survey, respondents were asked about reduction in the size of government employees; among the poor, low-caste and indigenous respondents who had an opinion, the majority was opposed to such reduction. The newly emergent, hitherto subordinate, social groups, often represented by primarily caste-based or regional parties, as they capture state power and reserved jobs, are not keen to give up the loaves and fishes of office or reduce the role of the public sector.

Of course, politicians have also done a poor job of explaining reforms to the common people. If it was clear that electricity reform, which may involve a higher price, but implies a higher capacity for the public utility to provide less erratic power supply, or that deregulation means loosening the grip of corrupt inspectors over small enterprises, some opposition could decline.

What financial columnists call anti-reform populism is actually a product of the manifold inequalities and conflicts of Indian society. Data on inequality of household wealth distribution and that between the educated and uneducated classes suggest, along with the prevailing caste and other social inequalities, that India is one of the most unequal countries in the world. Severe educational inequality, worse in India than in Brazil, for example, makes it harder for many to absorb shocks in the industrial labour market, since education and training could provide some means of flexibility in adapting to market changes.

China, for example, was able to weather the disruptions and hardships of restructuring under a more intense process of global integration during the 1980s and 1990s due to its minimum rural safety net. This security was largely made possible by an egalitarian distribution of land-cultivation rights that followed the de-collectivisation of 1978. In most parts of India, the poor have no similar rural safety net. So the resistance to the competitive process that market reform entails is that much stiffer in India.

In general, because of social heterogeneity and economic inequality, the social and political environment in India is conflict-ridden, and it is difficult in this environment to build consensus and organise collective action toward long-term reform and cooperative problem-solving efforts. When groups do not trust one another in the sharing of costs and benefits of long-run reform, there is the inevitable tendency to go for the "bird-in-hand" short-run subsidies and government handouts, which pile up as an enormous fiscal burden. Few politicians dare oppose the continuing serious under-pricing of water and electricity, the over-manning of the public payroll, and a longstanding refusal to tax the wealthiest farmers.

Economic nationalism of the right as well as the left parties has long resisted the inflow of large-scale foreign investment in India, which despite some increase in the last few years remains a small fraction of that in China. The fear in India— sometimes stoked by domestic companies keen to avert competition—is of large global companies manipulating venal Indian politicians and generally compromising political sovereignty. This is in line with the old "dependency theory" of development sociology, where underdevelopment is explained by foreign capital sapping the strength of domestic capital and the state. Ironically, China has turned "dependency theory" upside down: The regime seems more confident of controlling foreign than domestic private capital, and the latter is still discriminated against in terms of credit allocation and expansion of production outside local areas.

Issues of fiscal and trade policy, financial markets and capital-account convertibility preoccupy any discussion of economic reform. Reform would gain popularity if it were equally and simultaneously concerned with reform in the appalling governance structure in the delivery of basic social and infrastructural services for the poor in large parts of the country—in education, health, drinking water, irrigation and more. In the euphoria with the high growth rates of recent years, one should not forget, for example, that the atrocious condition in India's health sector is worse than that in even some African countries—for example, the percentage of underweight children in India is not just five times that in China, it is worse than most African countries. Resistance to market reforms also comes from environmentalists and those concerned with the rights of urban squatters, the indigenous and other marginalised people. Markets and development in general, have become identified with uprooting the livelihoods of the poorest people and despoliation of the environment. The record of resettlement and rehabilitation of people displaced by roads or dams or mining projects is dismal in India (it is, of course, worse in China), and recent history of such projects is replete with arbitrary land acquisitions, contractor fraud and broken promises to the poor.

The pro-reform people usually do not engage in the arguments about the narrowness of the development goals being pursued, except by just referring to the standard trickle-down process of growth. There are serious differences on the empirical judgment on the adequacy of growth trickle-down. In particular, employment growth at the low-skill levels has been disappointing so far, and to blame this on the restrictive labour laws, applicable to the large factory sector, is asking the tail to wag too large a dog, particularly in a country where more than 80 per cent of workers even in the non-agricultural sector work in informal activities where labour laws do not apply.

The opposition to economic reform thus reflects not just the lingering nostalgia for old-style Fabian socialism that the financial press likes to lampoon. The roots go much deeper, into the various distributive conflicts throughout Indian society.

PS: The results of the last (2014) national elections have sometimes been interpreted as a mandate for economic reforms. I have my doubts.

CHAPTER 2

On the New Land Acquisition Bill

Ideas for India, April 2013

INTRODUCTION[1]

The last decade has witnessed increasing unrest over land acquisition all over the country. The colonial era Land Acquisition Act of 1894 still serves as the legal basis for eminent domain, a few minor amendments notwithstanding. For the last two years, the United Progressive Alliance II Government has been preparing to introduce a new Land Acquisition Bill in Parliament. The Bill, initially drafted by the National Advisory Council, seems to have evolved quite a bit as it passed through the Cabinet, Standing Committee, and consultation with opposition parties. While details may yet change, some broad features will probably remain same.

Compensation to landowners must be a multiple of the local market price for land, as determined by the collector from recent sale deeds and circle rates. The multiplication factor has been changed several times and latest documents indicate it will be two times in urban areas and three times in rural areas (including the 100 per cent solatium). Since the current law requires compensation to equal market price, this is a significant increase.

---

1   Introduction by *Ideas for India*

Landowners as well as livelihood losers—families who earned their living from the land being acquired such as sharecroppers and agricultural labourers—are entitled to a relief and rehabilitation (R&R) package. The package consists of lump sum payments as well as other benefits, such as employment and land-for-land in the case of "urban development" projects. Industries are obligated to pay R&R even if they buy land through the market whenever the total acquisition is above a certain size.

Tougher procedural requirements will come into effect if the Bill becomes law. For example, "social impact assessment" has to be carried out by government committees before acquisition can go ahead. When private industries or PPP (public-private-partnership) projects acquire land above a minimum size, consent of at least 80 per cent of the affected population will be required.

Taken at face value, the Bill attempts to restrict eminent domain to projects with a "public purpose". It also makes noises about limiting the acquisition of multi-cropped land for reasons of food security but choice of ceilings will probably be left to states. Existing law has similar restrictions but in practice, they are rendered weak by provisions like the "urgency clause", which have been used quite liberally. Whether the restrictions in the new Bill will have more bite is a debatable issue.

A copy of the Bill can be downloaded from the Ministry of Rural Development's website (http://rural.nic.in/sites/downloads/general/LS%20Version%20of%20LARR%20%20Bill.pdf). However, this is an older version, which has undergone revisions and amendments.

Will the new Land Acquisition Bill make protests like those in Singur and Bhatta-Parsaul a thing of the past? Will it make land acquisition so expensive and difficult that the pace of industrialisation will suffer? Will it achieve justice? Development? Neither?

AUTHOR'S ANSWERS TO QUESTIONS

Q: In the last several years, attempts to acquire agricultural land for development projects have triggered protests and violence all over the country. The resistance seems to cut across states, ruling parties and the nature of projects (whether infrastructure or industry, mining or education, private, public or PPP). In your view, what are the endemic flaws in our current law and practice regarding land acquisition?

A: The 1894 Law is regarded by most people as obsolete, unfair, and hopelessly inadequate. In the last few years, we have been going through the travails of shaping a new Act that can address the conflicting demands of the various interests involved. The endemic flaws of the existing law and practice involve matters relating to due process, the extent of state involvement and coercion, adequate compensation and rehabilitation etc.

Q: Should eminent domain be used to acquire land for private industry (as is often the case under current law), or should industrialists be required to buy all the land they need from the market? If you take it at face value, the new Bill seems to restrict the practice, but critics have argued that it leaves enough loopholes for it to continue. What is your reading?

A: While people have been justifiably outraged by the arbitrariness and insensitivity with which the state has often applied the principle of 'eminent domain', this does not, in my judgment, negate the case for an appropriate role of the state in acquiring land, even on behalf of private industry. The state has to get involved for various reasons:

   (a) Particularly in the densely populated parts of the country, the number of tiny land owners is so large that the transaction costs in negotiation can be simply prohibitive from the point of view of the private companies. (This is in addition to the 'hold-up problem' by some recalcitrant seller that is usually given as rationale for 'eminent domain' in most countries.) Left to the market, the companies will turn to brokers and other middlemen, who in the common Indian experience of restrictive or sharp practices, may often exploit the small land-seller. Worse cases of strong-arm tactics by the land mafia are not unknown, and the state may have to actively intervene in preventing this.

(b) Even if the land-seller wants to negotiate directly, land records are often defective and contentious, and in the absence of title insurance, the land-buyers will feel more assured in the transaction if the state acquires it for them.

(c) In direct negotiations between the land buyers and sellers, without involvement of any third party, the tiny land-seller may be at a considerable disadvantage in bargaining with a large corporate buyer.

(d) The state has to be in any case involved in providing the minimum infrastructure (roads, power and water supply etc) for the private company, particularly if there is competition with other states in the matter of adequate supporting infrastructure.

(e) The state may also have to be involved in organising training and skill formation programmes for the people giving up their land—just promising them jobs, irrespective of qualifications, in the new projects, as is sometimes proposed, is unfair to the employers and inefficient for the economy.

(f) The state (including the local government at the village level) has to play a major role to ensure that the other livelihood-losers from the land sale (tenants, landless workers, rights holders under the Forest Rights Act etc) are provided for.

Of course, state officials, politicians and bureaucrats, are often corrupt, and may sometimes have lost trust of the people to do the right thing on a sensitive issue like land, and land acquisition becomes a matter of political football among rival political parties, as it has been in West Bengal. The whole matter of land transfer, administering of compensation and resettlement may have to be handed over to an independent quasi-judicial authority or regulatory commission, sufficiently insulated from the day-to-day political process but subject to periodic legislative review. The commission should regularly hold local hearings where all parties can present their cases and grievances. At the same time regulatory capture by real estate interests has to be guarded against.

Q: Much of the human displacement and suffering in post-independence India can be attributed to large public projects like dams, railways, highways, etc. The new Bill exempts many such projects from its provisions, while subjecting private industry to strict consent requirements and R&R obligations, even when it buys land from the market. Do you think the state is justified in imposing conditions on the private sector that it itself refuses to meet?

A: The consent and R&R requirements should be there for public infrastructure projects, but maybe in a less stringent form than in the case of land for private companies. In spite of all the displacements in the past, lack of adequate public infrastructure remains the major constraint for Indian economic development (including for private investment).

Q: Some people have raised concerns that the rapid conversion of agricultural land will have an adverse impact on agricultural output and food security. Do you think the new Bill addresses this concern adequately?

A: One should not exaggerate the food security issue, important though as it is. In most states, the amount of agricultural land that will be required for acquisition for infrastructure or industrial needs is a very small fraction. Also, not all states have comparative advantage in agriculture. Within a country, if the existing cumbersome restrictions on agricultural trade and distribution are relaxed, there should be considerable scope for getting food grains from other states. In any case, the new Bill proposes acquiring multi-crop land only as "a last resort".

Q: Current law provides some protection to land owners, but it leaves livelihood losers (such as tenants, sharecroppers and day labourers who work on the land) to fend for themselves. The R&R provisions of the new Bill have been extended to such stakeholders at least on paper, but do you think it has done enough to both identify and compensate this group?

A: I think the livelihood losers should be given a form of unemployment benefits for a specified period (or jobs, if they are qualified). Identifying the genuine cases of the eligible people is a tricky task in which the panchayats and gram sabha should be mobilised.

Q: In recent times, environmental regulation and mining activity have often cut off tribals' access to their traditional forest habitat. By most accounts, implementation of the Forest Rights Act of 2006 remains poor. How can the Land Acquisition Bill protect the interest of tribals? To be entitled to compensation and rehabilitation, one has to have secure property rights in the first place.

A: In the displacements of land acquisition in post-Independence India, tribal people have been the largest losers, and so one has to be especially cautious. This history is also littered with reneged promises of resettlement and repair of environmental damages. The new Bill is on the right track when it proposes that the compensation and rehabilitation of displaced people should precede the launching of any project (and the tribal people preferably resettled in the same Scheduled Area). There should also be some mechanism for punishing those officials (and companies they collude with) who systematically break promises. At the same time, the fear of displacing tribal people should not block all development projects some of which will, at least partially, benefit the same people with jobs and infrastructure. In the case of private mineral and other companies, some of their shares should be vested in a community fund (or the local panchayat treasury).

Q: The formula for compensating landowners has been set at some multiple of the market price. In the latest communication from the Ministry of Rural Development, we learn that compensation must be double in urban areas (if you count the 100 per cent solatium) and up to 3 times in rural areas (again, counting the solatium). Do you think this will do justice to farmers, and at the same time, keep the price of acquisition sensible?

A: Compensation is probably the most contentious issue. The fixing of the compensation multiplier has to keep several things in mind:

(i) It has to be large enough for voluntary sales but low enough for keeping the new project viable. As is widely known, in the last few years land prices in urban and semi-urban India have gone up excessively in many areas (often in speculative spirals), so the multiplier may have to be re-adjusted accordingly.

(ii) The new Bill proposes to give flexibility to the state governments, but too much flexibility may lead to race-to-the-bottom competition between states to attract industrialists.

(iii) Instead of pre-fixed multipliers, the idea of land auctions at the panchayat level seems attractive particularly from the point of view of reflecting heterogeneity of land values and offers. However, given the low state capacity and high official corruptibility at that level, chances of capture of the process by brokers and middlemen, pre-emptive land-buying by them, and bid rigging are large. Maybe, some area-wise land value indices for different agro-climatic zones in the country (keeping in mind broad variations in soil quality and water access) should be pre-announced (like those used in many cities in India for municipal property assessment, though agricultural land may be more heterogeneous than urban property), and any bidding should be within those parameters.

Even if we all agree on compensation multipliers, this will still keep another source of farmer dissatisfaction unresolved. I would call this ex post dissatisfaction, after the sales transaction, when the seller sees unanticipated price rise of land (particularly, if he had sold it to the middlemen and brokers who become active in buying land from farmers long before the proposal for a new factory or a road is mooted), which the former have missed out and which is being enjoyed by their fellow villagers who did not have to sell their land. Recent agitations in UP and Haryana on this issue turned to violence.

One solution is for the state to offer sellers a compensation package in two parts.

- A lump-sum amount related to the current market value of the agricultural land (adjusted by the multiplier discussed above); and,
- An annuity (a monthly pension, as it were, for the farmer's retirement) from a trust fund where some shares of the new company are vested.

This fund will collect shares from all companies in the business of buying land all over the state, so that risks are pooled on a large scale without the fund brought down by any particular project failure. The fund should be independently and professionally managed (like pension funds in many countries). From the point of view of financial security, a stream of annuity payments may be much better for poor farmers than one-off cash payments. Of course, since it will be something new, extensive information campaigns explaining the nature of annuity to the people should be arranged. In projects where the land is acquired mainly for public infrastructure, and no such company shares are relevant, a betterment levy on nearby land may be contributed to the trust fund. In the case of mining projects, the mining rights should be auctioned in a transparently competitive bidding process, and the proceeds are to be deposited in this trust fund for annuity payments to the dispossessed.

CHAPTER 3

Hear that Hollow in the Drumbeat?

Outlook, 28 April 2014

The drumbeats are all around us, proclaiming the triumphal arrival of Narendra Modi as our next prime minister. They are already reaching deafening proportions among urban middle classes, NRIs and the corporate sector-owned media. For the last few months, a rising crescendo of clamour about a 'Modi wave' has, through clever PR and slick advertisements along with his gruff eloquence and prodigious energy, indeed created in a self-reinforcing way a wave about the 'unstoppability' of a supreme leader. The myths building around him are now almost impenetrable. Yet a close scrutiny of them is worthwhile even if he is to become the next PM.

Modi has made governance the major plank of his platform, and through constant repetition, his excellent record in this respect is now taken as a given fact in many quarters. There is no doubt that much that is wrong in Indian politics has to do with governance issues at all levels. Modi has pointed to his record of strong and quick decisions in his state of Gujarat and its superb performance in economic growth, which he now promises to replicate for the rest of India.

Governance has both political and economic dimensions, let us discuss both. The 2002 massacres in Gujarat that happened under Modi's watch suggest a disastrous governance failure. Even if his personal complicity is not legally established (partly because of destroyed evidence), there is no question that horrendous things happened under his watch in an administration he firmly controlled (he was not just a backseat passenger in the car when, sadly, a "puppy got run over"). Some of his close associates have either been indicted or are currently under investigation. The then prime minister of his own party, Atal Behari Vajpayee, rebuked Modi at the time for deviating from his 'rajdharma' (the Sanskrit word for good governance).

Modi's supporters say that Muslims are better-off in Gujarat than in poorer states like Bihar. This is like white Afrikaners in the Apartheid regime saying that Blacks were economically better-off in South Africa than in Nigeria. Robbed of their dignity and security, Muslims who used to live across different parts of Ahmedabad are now huddled in squalid ghettos on the fringes of the city.

Modi's well-funded and efficient campaign machine has successfully deflected public attention away from all this to his Gujarat model of economic governance. Occasionally his mask slips, and he talks about the rise in 'meat exports' under Congress rule from the slaughterhouses mainly run by you know who, or about a 'conspiracy' to kill rhinos in Assam in order to give space for Bangladeshis to settle in, about his political opponents being 'Pakistani agents', and so on. But, in general, he keeps to the theme of economy and strong India, while delegating the job of hate and fear-mongering to his minions, particularly in the all-important states of Uttar Pradesh and Bihar. The BJP politicians implicated in the Muzaffarnagar riots have been given tickets in this election and Amit Shah has reportedly called for "revenge" against "those who have been ill-treating our mothers and sisters".

In economic governance, there is no doubt that Modi has done some good things for the Gujarat economy. His electricity reform, for instance, has been exemplary. He, of course, exaggerates Gujarat's relative economic performance under him, but what is more surprising is how easily this is accepted by even his non-admirers. Studies show—see, for example, the piece by Maitreesh Ghatak and Sanchari Roy in a recent issue of this magazine (*A Look in the Mirror*, 31 March 2014)—that a few other states have done even better compared to the national average in the first decade of this century relative to the 1990s, in both economic growth (for example, Maharashtra) and poverty reduction (for example, Tamil Nadu). Thirty years back, Gujarat was No. 2 among Indian states in industrial development, and under Modi it has remained No. 2. Even in industrial growth, much of it in recent years has been in the petroleum refineries sector, which is highly capital-intensive and creates very few jobs for common people. In the delivery of basic social services (health, nutrition, education, etc), the performance of many other states (for example, Tamil Nadu and Himachal Pradesh) has been substantially better. Taking growth and social welfare together, the best development performance in the last decade or so has been in Tamil Nadu. So even though at public platforms Modi likes to thump his 56-inch chest as 'Vikaspurush' (Mr Development), some of it is really hype.

The Indian corporate sector is tirelessly promoting this glittering image of Modi. The reasons have much to do with the reputation he has of giving generous business subsidies—capital subsidies and corporate tax concessions given by his government amount to several times the subsidies for food and agriculture—and the way he 'decisively' rides roughshod over business hindrances like clearances on environment and land acquisition. Modi is eloquent against the Congress government's programmes of 'dole' for the poor, but his reformist friends among economists ignore that his corporate welfare payments suggest that he is business-friendly, but not necessarily market-friendly. Many critics who refer to Modi's crony capitalism point to the disproportionately sharp rise over recent weeks in the stock prices (unwarranted by the fundamentals) of particular business groups close to him.

Along with the hype, there is also a bit of naivety in the public enthusiasm for him. It is not clear that if he takes over the leadership in Delhi, he will be able to ram through his economic programmes in the face of the formidable structural (political, bureaucratic, institutional) problems that face any reform-minded government in India. The country as a whole is far too complex and poor compared to Gujarat, which has been business-friendly and advanced in both governance and physical infrastructure (like roads, ports, etc) over many decades now. On top of this, Modi's rather high-handed autocratic personal style (which is resented by many even within his own party) does not augur well for the intricate negotiations with diverse groups, state leaders and coalition partners he will necessarily have to work with at the all-India level. His polarising personality is not conducive to the tasks of compromise and consensus-building a leader inevitably faces in a highly fragmented polity like India's.

Another common position popular among some Indian journalists is that Indian democracy will ultimately 'tame' Modi, the checks and balances in our system will smooth his rough edges over time. First of all, our democratic institutions are not all that strong. Our elections are vigorous, but other essential parts of a democracy, like some basic human rights and certain regular procedures of accountability are fragile, even after all these years. One should not welcome further pressures on these institutions and procedures just for trying out a firebrand leader; in any case the hankering for a strong leader that our middle classes display, while it may be understandable after a decade of ineffective, inarticulate and jaded Congress leadership, is not exactly healthy. Middle classes in South Europe and South America have often gone through such phases of hankering, with disastrous consequences. Our democracy is also decidedly weak at the local level (districts and below) in most parts of India, and most political parties have no inner-party democracy, with major decisions mainly taken from above. In such a situation, a leader given to propensities for aggregation and concentration of power is potentially harmful to democratic processes. After the chaotic '90s Russian hankering for a strong leader has given them, through landslide elections, Vladimir Putin, who has turned Russia into a cesspool of oligarchic corruption and human rights abuse.

Of course, Modi has cultivated an image of a fighter against corruption, and this is welcomed by people tired of one scam after another during the Congress regime (revealed ironically with the help of one of that regime's landmark legislations, the Right to Information Act). But at the same time nothing has stopped him from trying to reabsorb into the party some of the leaders in Karnataka associated with the egregious cases of corruption in real estate and mining. It is also well-known that some of the National Democratic Alliance chief ministers were complicit in the decisions around the coal scam. A couple of years back, the Comptroller and Auditor General of India had complained about serious financial mismanagement in the Gujarat public sector. Also, the crony capitalism that Modi indulges in is a form of corruption under the broad definition of corruption as abuse of public office, which need not always be illegal.

Above all, with a history of inter-community relations as fraught as in India and the discovery by Modi and his party over the years that, if necessary, mobilising fear and hatred among the majority community can pay good electoral dividends, it is not always clear how merely the periodic electoral check of democracy can tame a leader who is equally adept at playing the development and the communal cards. Facing roadblocks on his way, he can turn either way, the explosive consequences of which in our fractured society, where violence is often just below the surface, Modi may not be able to control. One, of course, hopes this will not happen, but Modi's history and background do not comfort us.

CHAPTER 4

The Labour Reform Myth

The Indian Express, 23 August 2014

Many economists and businessmen regard the reform of labour law as vital for the proposed revival of the manufacturing sector in India. In a widely noted move, the Rajasthan Government has already taken a step towards amending Chapter VB of the Industrial Disputes Act, 1947 (IDA), raising the exemption limit in the law that restricts laying off workers without government permission to firms with more than 300 workers. The Haryana Government has also indicated similar intentions. Such experimentations at the state level, particularly when the implementation of labour laws is in the hands of state governments, are in principle a step in the right direction. But there are reasons to believe that if people expect big changes in output and employment simply as a result of such reforms, they may be in for a big disappointment.

First, it is not clear that the rigid law on retrenchment is always the binding constraint on manufacturing expansion. Take the highly labour-intensive garments industry, for example. A combined dataset (for formal-sector firms from the Annual Survey of Industries and informal-sector firms from the National Sample Survey) shows that about 92 per cent of garment firms in India have fewer than eight employees (the bunching of firms is around the eight-employee size, not the below-100-employee size, as one would have expected). Labour law cannot discourage an eight-employee firm from expanding to an 80-employee firm since Chapter VB of the IDA does not kick in until the firm reaches the size of 100 employees. So the binding constraints on the expansion of that eight-employee firm may have to do with inadequate credit and marketing opportunity, erratic power supply, wretched roads, bureaucratic regulations etc. There are good statistical studies by some economists which show that states with more rigid labour laws have had lower industrial growth and that labour laws can be a constraint. But these studies do not show that they are the only or even the main constraint. I do not know of a single statistical study or growth decomposition exercise in India that shows the relative dominance of the labour law constraint over other constraints. By constantly repeating the same objection about labour laws, some people may be barking up the wrong tree.

Second, Rajasthan is not the first state to relax Chapter VB. Gujarat relaxed it for Special Economic Zones (SEZ) in 2004, Andhra Pradesh did so in 2006. Uttar Pradesh's 1983 relaxation, which remained in force for 20 years, applied to the whole state—it raised the exemption limit to what Rajasthan is proposing now. I have not seen any serious study of the effects of these relaxations on job creation. Contrary to the recent election propaganda, the Gujarat model of development has not been particularly exemplary on continued job creation. A large part of its high manufacturing growth has been in petrochemicals and refineries, which are highly capital intensive. Does anyone believe that the UP relaxation for nearly 20 years led to a great many manufacturing jobs? If that did not happen, it may be largely due to the other constraints mentioned above. At an all-India level, why is it that the large and high-growth service sector has led to such little job growth (outside construction) over the last two decades? The IDA applies to industries, not to the service sector.

Third, over the decades, how many states have really strictly followed the labour laws? There are many cases of a state government looking the other way when they are violated. An important part of labour laws in India is the Contract Labour (Regulation and Abolition) Act, 1970 which restricts employment of short-term workers without benefits. Yet, it is well known that this act remains mostly on paper. According to an estimate based on Annual Survey of Industries data by A Sood, P Nath, and S Ghosh in "Deregulating Capital, Regulating Labour" (*Economic & Political Weekly*, 28 June 2014), in 2009-10, about half of the workers in factories with more than 5,000 workers were employed through contractors. In factories employing between 100 and 5,000 workers, more than a quarter were contract workers. Similarly, an estimate from National Sample Survey data suggest that in 2011-12, about 80 per cent of workers in organised manufacturing either had no written job contracts or the contract was for less than one year. All this has clearly given employers a great deal of flexibility. If Indian labour laws were really that stringent in practice, how is it that during the downturn around 2008, nearly one million workers quickly lost their jobs in labour-intensive export sectors?

I am actually very much in favour of labour law reform. I would even support abolishing the firm size limit on retrenchment altogether, provided there is a provision for adequate unemployment benefits. Allowing more flexibility in hiring and firing has to be combined with a reasonable scheme of unemployment compensation from an earmarked fund, to which employers as well employees should regularly contribute. No Indian politician has yet gathered the courage or imagination to come up with such a package deal. More importantly, the whole gamut of Indian labour laws requires a major overhaul, not just Chapter VB of the IDA. The Trade Unions Act, 1926, allowing any seven workers to form a union, rampant union rivalry and lack of recognised trade unions as negotiating agents etc have led to a highly fragmented labour movement and a chaotic shop floor. More than 10 years back, the Second National Commission on Labour made some useful recommendations to change this state of affairs, but they remained mostly unimplemented. Meanwhile, there are some changes afoot in the grassroots Indian labour scene. While some businessmen continue to think in an adversarial way of "flexibility" as being "union-free", there are new kinds of party-independent unions (for example, the New Trade Union Initiative), which are trying to mediate in the shaping and sustaining of labour-friendly practices that are compatible with global competitiveness and high productivity. Instead of constantly repeating the same mantra about Chapter VB, the Indian policy community should think of imaginative overall reforms that may help both labour and capital.

CHAPTER 5

Replacing the Planning Commission

Ideas for India, 11 September 2014

[In his address to the nation, from the ramparts of the Red Fort on India's 68th Independence Day, Prime Minister Modi announced his government's decision to abolish the Planning Commission:

"I believe that when Planning Commission was constituted, it was done on the basis of the circumstances and the needs of those times ... but the prevalent situation in the country is different, global scenario has also changed, governments are no longer the Centre of economic activities, the scope of such activities has broadened... therefore within a short period, we will replace the planning commission with a new institution having a new design and structure, a new body, a new soul, a new thinking, a new direction, a new faith towards forging a new direction to lead the country based on creative thinking, public-private partnership, optimum utilisation of resources, utilisation of youth power of the nation, to promote the aspirations of state governments seeking development, to empower the state governments and to empower the federal structure."

The Planning Commission performed the following functions:

a. Preparation of the Plan Document
b. Allocation of funds between: (a) states and centre; and (b) central ministries
c. Appraisal of all expenditures of the central ministries
d. Mediating between states and central government
e. Providing independent opinion on all project/ programme proposals of central ministries
f. Monitoring progress of central government schemes
g. Mediating between central ministries on issues of a crosscutting nature[1]]

In view of the above;

Q: Of the functions which need to continue to be performed which should be retained in the new institution and which can be located in other existing bodies? Reasons may please be provided.

A: (i) The allocation of all funds between the states and the centre should be largely handed over to the Finance Commission, which needs to be a permanent body (with membership regularly rotated) instead of being periodically appointed. The mandatorily appointed State Finance Commissions (often disregarded or rendered dysfunctional in reality) should decide on allocations between the state government, panchayats and municipal bodies, and should be institutionally linked up with the national Finance Commission.

(ii) The negotiations and deliberations on inter-state issues (including allocations) should be done at the Constitution–mandated Inter-State Council (already in existence since 1990), suitably rejuvenated. This body is the appropriate forum for meaningful discussions on the 'federal structure'. The permanent Finance Commission should have regular interchange with this Council before announcing their periodic allocations.

---

1 Introduction by *Ideas for India*

(iii)The allocation of funds among central ministries should be the responsibility of the Ministry of Finance.

(iv)Appraisal of expenditures and evaluation of programmes should be done by a permanent Expenditure Commission in collaboration with a permanent Independent Evaluation Office.

Q: Are there other (new) functions that should be performed by the new institution? Please specify with reasons.

A: Nostalgia for the glory days of the Planning Commission or the largely false cliché that a market economy does not need planning should both be avoided. A statutory body replacing the Planning Commission should be called something like the Long-Term Development Commission (LTDC). Its main functions will be to:

(a) study the long-term investment goals of different sectors of the economy in terms of a coherent framework of the economy as a whole;

(b) sort out inconsistencies and trade-offs in moving towards such goals;

(c) work out the modalities of balancing conflicting objectives for large projects—for example, how to reconcile the often conflicting needs of high growth, environmental challenges, job creation, macroeconomic stability, keeping the rise in social, economic and regional inequalities in check, etc;

[Let me elaborate a bit on this need for balancing with an illustration. Caught in the cross-fire between corporate lobbies, real estate and mining tycoons on the one hand and social activists and judiciary on the other, in recent years official land and environmental clearances for infrastructure and other development projects have become extremely slow, non-transparent or erratic (lurching from one side to the other—in the current regime the signs are that it will now lurch to one extreme). Under the circumstances it is imperative to have an expert body, beholden to neither side, which will carefully and transparently examine the merits and demerits on both sides and come to a balanced assessment of the social costs and benefits for each major project and make that assessment publicly available.]

(d) formulate 'indicative' 20-year plans on issues particularly requiring broad long-term visions—like those relating to the looming problems of energy, water, urban infrastructure and climate change; and,

(e) work on the conceptual and design problems of a coordinated and comprehensive programme for social protection for the citizens.

Q: In order to perform the functions envisaged for the new institution, what should be its legal position, character and structure? What should be the composition and staffing of the new institution?

A: (i) LTDC, while doing a lot of wide-ranging and long-term thinking, MUST NOT be just a think tank, of which there are quite a few in Delhi. To get political attention, its head should be a member of the cabinet, where some of its occasional reports will be submitted and discussed. The cabinet then should present to the parliament a statement on what action has been taken on the basis of these reports.

(ii) In view of the on-going and somewhat unhealthy concentration of power in the Prime Minister's Office (PMO), it is important to ensure the independence of the LTDC to critically examine the long-term implications of all major government policies. In choosing the members of LTDC one has to keep in mind that the respectability of LTDC will depend on, apart from their expertise, their demonstrated ability to make critical judgments devoid of narrow partisanship.

The tenure of the members should be durable, and their critical examination of government policy should be open for discussion in the parliament and the media. The administrative staff of LTDC should not be transient like in the ministries; as befitting an organisation given to thinking long-term, one should devise ways to ensure their spending a large part of their career there.

(iii)If the Inter-state Council approves, there should be equivalents of LTDC at the state levels, and scope for regular communication and exchange of ideas between the LTDC's at different levels. The state-level body should be encouraged to carry out experiments and trial-and-error exercises on a small scale with new policies, the results of which could then be shared with the national body.

CHAPTER 6

The Avoidable Tragedy of the Left in India

Economic & Political Weekly, 11 June 2011

In the two decades since the collapse of the Soviet Union, the Left in India has not renewed itself. In the context of the electoral debacle in West Bengal and the defeat in Kerala, this article revisits the issue and asks, what future now for the Left in the country? The Left certainly has a role to play in India but to be able to do so it needs to pay attention to the many general issues that currently afflict it.

Almost exactly 20 years ago, around the time of the fall of the Soviet Union, I wrote a piece in this journal titled "The Avoidable Tragedy of the Left in India" (*Economic &Political Weekly*, 19 October 1991). I wish I could say that the Left has been wiser in the intervening period. I used to think that once the gerontocracy at the helm of the Left parties moved on, the younger leadership would be more innovative and imaginative. Unfortunately, some of the younger leaders who have since been at the helm have turned out to be even more unthinking, dogmatic, and dense. With "democratic centralism", which is mumbo jumbo for tyrannical control by the leadership, the Left parties have also disabled themselves from easy course correction. Even though I am writing this after the Left debacle in West Bengal, and the marginal defeat in Kerala, in this article, I will mostly talk about the general issues afflicting the Left, some of which, if paid serious attention to, can yet restore the legitimacy of what I believe to be a necessary role the Left can and should play in India.

SELF-DECEPTION

I am always struck by the amazing capacity of the Left parties for self-deception in the face of a crisis, avoidance of the hard realities and resort to clichés and solace from sacred texts. In the context of a fast-changing world, their policy pronouncements continue to be obsolete formulae-driven and marked by chanting of catechisms: Market bad, State good; public sector good, private bad; leftist unions even when they act in reactionary, anti-poor and highhanded ways have to be defended; in foreign policy, America bad, China, Russia good (even when the latter countries now display rampant oligarchic, crony capitalism), even the theocratic-authoritarian regime in Iran has to be supported because it fights the evil American empire, and so on.

In West Bengal, the resounding defeat of the Left Front, even with its history of considerable achievements in organising popular participation in meaningful land reform and rural decentralisation, is not just due to the peasant disaffection with its recent efforts at land acquisition, but more due to widely and intensely resented all-pervasive and oppressive party control of all aspects of local life. If you want a public hospital bed for your seriously ill family member, you have to be a supplicant with the local party boss; if you want to start a small business or be a street vendor you have to pay protection money to the party *dada*; if you want to ply a taxi or an auto-rickshaw you have to pay a tribute to the local party union; if you want a schoolteacher's job you have to be approved by the "local committee" and pay them an appropriate amount; your children are to go to schools where the union activist teacher is often absent, compelling you to pay good money in sending them to his private coaching classes; if you want to build a house you have to employ party-approved construction workers and buy higher priced or inferior-quality building materials from party-approved suppliers; if you want to buy land, you have to go through the party-connected "promoter", etc.

ALL-POWERFUL PARTY

In the name of Marxism the long-ruling party essentially became the all-powerful local mafia. Of course, in true godfather style they will often help you in emergencies, if you show your loyalty. This way of operating a party is not unique to West Bengal, the Shiv Sena does it all the time, but they do not add insult to injury by spouting revolutionary or anti-imperialist rhetoric, or chanting *Lal salam* even as they fleece or intimidate you, while the police nearby show studied indifference. The party leaders have a habitual way of explaining electoral defeats by saying that their cadres have "lost touch with the people"; the common people often wish they did.

LENINIST LEGACY

The overriding principle of supremacy of party control is a poisonous Leninist legacy, and its degeneration into local tyranny is a sad but inevitable consequence. The Leninist principle is often invoked for the sake of discipline. Apart from the Rashtriya Swayamsevak Sangh (RSS), the Communist Party of India (Marxist) [CPI(M)] used to be the most disciplined political organisation in the country. No more. While the tightness of control over dissenting opinion at the top continues, it has now become flabby and unruly below, and in many local areas run by extortionists over whom the top leadership has very little control. Hopefully, after the party's defeat in West Bengal and the subsequent end of police protection, the thugs will now look for greener pastures, and there is a chance now for the CPI(M) to cleanse itself. In the all-India context, the Left is now mainly effective as a lobby for public sector employees, and it occasionally flexes its muscles by calling bandhs (on a suitable Monday or Friday), which paralyse city life, give *babus* a long weekend, while starving the poor informal workers who depend for their daily livelihood on casual wage work or street vending. The image of the Left in the minds of the vast numbers of the poor is that of the union organiser for the corrupt or callous public employees whom they have to face as the potential recipients of the paltry delivery of basic social and administrative services.

FAILURE IN BASIC SERVICES

In the history of communist countries while governments have miserably failed in many aspects of the economy, at least in basic health and educational services they have often done a much better job than in non-communist countries at the same income level (China, Vietnam, Cuba are obvious examples). But this does not apply to West Bengal. The party organisation was solidly based on unionised schoolteachers, health workers, clerks and other public employees—and they used their union clout to default in the delivery of public services. The coddled bureaucracy was allowed to be lackadaisical, files moved much slower than in secretariats of many other states, and the culture of union-protected impunity for public employees (including the police) thrived. The appointments and promotions in colleges and universities, directly orchestrated from the party office in Alimuddin Street [CPI(M) Head Quarter in Kolkata] and screened for party loyalty, decimated Bengal's long-enjoyed advantage in academic, intellectual and professional pursuits.

INFORMAL SECTOR BYPASSED

A major failure of the Left in India is in not being able to organise, except in localised pockets, the overwhelming majority of workers who are informal, often self-employed.

The modes of organising these workers would have to be quite different: as home is often the workplace rather than concentrated centres like factory or office, wage or job security is not the main issue, welfare benefits and general economic security may be the more important ones, citizen rights may be more salient than worker rights, etc. Non-left non-government organisations with a citizen rights-based approach or Gandhian organisations (the most well-known of which is Self Employed Women's Association (SEWA), organising a trade union of self-employed women) have often been more successful in this area. There needs to be a major reorientation in Left thinking on labour issues in this direction. In general, Left thinking in India slurs over the contradictions within the labour movement (particularly between formal and informal workers) and the special organisational exigencies of the latter.

On land issues also the Left parties, which used to be at the forefront of movements, have largely run out of steam. First of all, on land distribution or tenurial security rights, the Left parties in both Kerala and West Bengal have found out in their bitter experience that peasants once having received those rights do not feel particularly obliged to continue to vote for the parties that originally won those rights for them.

In politics, gratitude for past once-for-all beneficial actions soon wears out. Second, particularly in West Bengal, over time small and middle farmer families have come to capture the rural leadership in the local party, and this has led to some weakening of the cause of agitating for the wage demands of landless workers; it is no coincidence that the wage rise of the latter hurts those farmers who hire labour. Third, in densely populated parts of India the land-man ratio is declining fast, pushing a large part of the land below the minimum viable cultivable unit. So earlier radical slogans like "land to the tiller" do not resonate as much. The Left should be active in organising some form of joint management in cultivation of tiny plots, particularly in matters of water, energy, knowledge of new agronomic practices and land nutrient inputs, and in marketing. But it is hardly active in these matters. The history of the cooperative movement in agriculture is dismal in India. Cooperatives, when they exist, more often than not have degenerated into moribund bureaucratic entities or front organisations for milking state subsidies, or occasionally captured by the rich and powerful (as in the case of sugar cooperatives of Maharashtra). The successful cases of cooperative organisations like the Gujarat Cooperative Milk Marketing Federation (Amul) have very little to do with the Left. Yet the importance of cooperative marketing will loom larger as Indian agriculture shifts from traditional grain to high-valued produce (like fruits, vegetables, livestock and dairy products). Lack of progress on this front will only bring about the dominance of large retail companies (with enough resources to invest in cold storage and transportation) and contract farming, which the Left in India often reflexively opposes (though the Chinese Party has gone for them in a big way). Fourth, as the productivity per person declines in agriculture and as its share in GDP gets very small, the overwhelming proportion of even farmers' children (there is survey evidence for this) want to get out of agriculture. Yet the transfer of land to other more productive uses has given rise to politically explosive protests in different parts of India. In the case of Nandigram and Singur, the attempts at land acquisition for industrial use has been resented by the people, partly because (a) the Left Front government (following largely the obsolete colonial law) offered inadequate compensation ; (b) unnecessarily and clumsily used force ; (c) the battle (at least in Nandigram) was less about land acquisition (the state government announced quite early in the process that no land will be acquired there) and more about turf warfare between CPI(M) and Trinamool goons—the Left government did little to control the gangland warfare; and (d) the long-term Left neglect of the backward state of education made many peasants concerned that their children will not be qualified to get any jobs in the new factories.

The Left now should not draw the wrong lessons from their electoral defeat, as some in the CPI(M) are already urging.

188 Globalisation, Democracy and Corruption: An Indian Perspective

Even after the bitter experience of the recent past, farmers may give up land voluntarily if they are offered a substantial share in the surplus that will be generated from the alternative use of land (say in the form of a steady annuity income, rather than cash that tends to get frittered away), if local participatory and deliberative processes are used to inform and involve them, if the annuity flow is administered by a credibly independent and efficient organisation, and if enough arrangements for skill formation and vocational training for farmers' children are made.

DISPOSSESSION AND DISPLACEMENT

Some within the CPI(M), and many to the left of the CPI(M) are understandably preoccupied with the general issue of dispossession and displacement effects of industrial and commercial development, particularly on the lives of the poor. Many of the abuses they point out are indeed egregious. There are difficult issues and trade-offs involved here. I can only make a plea for some balance between the need for economic development that creates productive jobs and enhances social surplus (which can potentially be redistributed) on the one hand, and on the other the need for minimising (and adequately compensating for) the dislocation by means of a process in which the local stakeholders can be full participants. The use of land and minerals by profit-seeking companies for non-traditional higher-productivity activities is in some ways historically indispensable (as Marx would have recognised) if we want any change in the miserable way of life that the peasants and *adivasis* have endured for centuries—as the Marxist economist Emmanuel once wrote, the horrors of capitalism fade in comparison with the horrors of pre-capitalism. There is too much romanticising of the traditional life among some otherwise well-intentioned activists (both of the Gandhian and far-left persuasion) and too little interest in assessing the complex trade-offs involved. On the other hand, in the current dispensation the surplus generated in the process of development in these areas is grossly inequitably distributed, much of it grabbed by the corporate oligarchy, real estate tycoons, the mining mafia, and their political patrons and collaborators. We have to find a balanced, equitable, and sustainable way of dividing the surplus and minimising the loss (both private and social, including environmental). In this the democratic Left (as opposed to the misguided and violent extreme Left) can play a valuable role in espousing the cause of the deprived, increasing their awareness and information, catalysing their organisations and acting as watchdogs against the abuses of state violence and corporate power.

ASSOCIATIONAL LIFE

One important difference between Kerala and West Bengal is the much richer associational life in Kerala's society, with a long history of literacy and solidarity movements for low caste emancipation, people's science movements, civic organisations (including those related to churches) and, of course, a strong set of Left-led organisations of landless workers and small peasants. Civil society is much weaker in West Bengal, in spite of strong unions of clerks, schoolteachers and peasants (industrial unions are weak and demoralised in a string of declining sunset industries). Associational life has been largely hijacked by the party, explicitly discouraging the growth of non-party civic organisations in its shadow. There are some lower caste associations (like those of the "matua" group, which the party in its desperation before the elections tried to appease, too late), but unlike in other states they have been marginal to the *bhadralok*-led politics. While bhadraloks presided in the upper echelons of the party, the lower level operatives used the party dominance to arm themselves and create their little mafia fiefdoms, which thrived with the neutered police looking away. In the absence of robust civic organisations, the local-level politics quickly fell into a vortex of violence. The Trinamool Congress fought an uphill battle with its own squads of goons, and finally won with the headwind of accumulated popular disgust at the tyranny of party control and peasant anxiety about their land. But decentralisation which is supposed to have been a success in West Bengal should have provided a local-democratic arena for resolving conflicts and a check to the violence. While panchayats in West Bengal have not been captured by the landed oligarchy (as in many other states) largely on account of the prior land reform, and some of the welfare benefit programmes did reach sections of the poor, local governments are weak in terms of finance which mostly comes from above and local elections are fought not so much on local issues but more on state-level partisan issues. Benefits often went to sections of the poor who were in a clientelistic relationship with the ruling party. So the panchayats became just one more arena for bitter partisan battles, usually around the allocation of the scanty doles from above, from state-supported or centrally-sponsored schemes. Kerala panchayats have been given a lot more finance by the state government, decentralised planning is more participatory, and in some districts there is even a record of municipal governments running business enterprises (in collaboration with local private business and voluntary organisations)—something practically non-existent in West Bengal.

On MARKET REFORM

Finally, the Left parties have to give up on their blatant hypocrisy on market reform. The reform policies pursued in Delhi are routinely described as "neo-liberal", supposedly adopted under imperialist and World Bank influence, while basically similar policies are followed in Kolkata, Agartala or Thiruvananthapuram. Just as many decades back, after long and acrimonious debates, the communist parties in India reconciled to working under "bourgeois democracy", they have to reconcile themselves to the market principle. These are both about competition, one in the polity, and the other in the economy. Markets have a large number of well recognised problems: market "failures" in resource allocation on account of externalities and imperfect information, inequalities that markets tend to facilitate, the instability, unemployment, and the economic and cultural dislocation that they often bring about, etc. But there are ways of mitigating these negative effects. The alternative to markets is often worse. The history of socialist countries has shown us repeatedly how without competition among producers and a mechanism for exit of chronically inefficient firms, no economy can attain or retain its vigour and dynamism. Political or bureaucratic allocation of resources and control of prices often lead to corruption, black markets and stagnation. The inequality in wealth in socialist countries is between the privileged members of the party oligarchy (and their accomplices) and the rest, and unemployment takes the form of low-productivity "disguised unemployment". Barring utopian projects on the drawing board of many wishful thinkers, no one has yet shown us in practice a consistently and durably viable and technologically dynamic economy for a large enough country that has been run on traditional socialist lines of controls and state monopoly. The socialist economies of Eastern Europe and Russia collapsed largely on their own endogenous systemic weakness. Common people in capitalist South Korea are immeasurably better off than in socialist near-starvation North Korea (which started off with an initial industrial advantage over the South). For three decades now China has deliberately attempted following a comprehensive policy of state-guided capitalism (adapting the models in South Korea, Taiwan, Singapore, and earlier Japan for their own circumstances) and has succeeded famously. In many respects Chinese policy has been much more "neo-liberal" than Indian. Vietnam is following policies similar to China.

POSSIBLE PRIORITIES

I think the Left should concentrate on leading popular struggles against capitalist excesses and injustices (rampant inequality and the consequent capture of political processes, displacement of poor people, macroeconomic instability—most recently due to short-sighted recklessness of unregulated financial markets abroad, and environmental degradation). The required systemic modifications and regulations will not make the capitalists happy, but through democratic pressures one can work out a bargaining arrangement in which the social justice objectives are vigorously pursued, but the incentives for production and surplus generation are not hurt too much; and state and community-level coordination mechanisms are used to cope with various kinds of coordination failures in the economy without substantially giving up on the important coordinating and disciplining functions of the market. Such a bargaining equilibrium may or may not be called "social democracy"—a term which raises suspicion in many on the Left, while many on the liberal side smell too much socialism in it. Forgetting about the well-known European examples, even among developing countries, in Latin America a small country, Costa Rica, has a thriving democracy with a superb system of welfare benefits for the masses; in a large country, Brazil, under the Workers' Party the erstwhile high inequality is going down (their index of income inequality is now about the same as in China), and education and health services have advanced a great deal and they are aiming at a form of social democracy, without giving up on the capitalist features of production. The Indian situation is, of course, different, but there are many international examples now to learn from (particularly in regulations and in provision of social services) and adapt to our circumstances. Even within India, a non-Left state like Tamil Nadu has advanced in the last three decades much more than West Bengal under the Left, both in industrialisation and in delivery of social services. Kerala, of course, has been on top in terms of social services for many decades, both under Left and non-Left rule, but its production system has not been dynamic enough, and it is more of a remittance economy. In general, the Left has to think hard why it is now only a regional party, and why even in its regions of strength it is getting weaker. When Marx in his last years was learning about Russian data and special conditions, he was quite open to changing his long-held ideas formed from his study of West European history (as he explicitly indicated to some of his correspondents), much to the consternation of some of his faithful followers. Sticking to old dogmas in the face of changing reality and new information is definitely un-Marxian.

CHAPTER 7

Our Self-Righteous Civil Society

Economic & Political Weekly, 16 July 2011

In chapter 6, I wrote on the structural and ideological impasse, various self-inflicted wounds and the organisational imperatives facing the Left parties in India. But over the last few decades in Indian public space, the non-party volunteer organisations have been much more effective in social movements and more articulate in policy debates than the traditional Left parties. In this essay, while recognising their manifold achievements I reflect on the serious limitations of the activities of the voluntary sector, and argue that when they usurp certain roles they can become a threat to representative democracy. I emphasise why in spite of the latter's prominence, the Left parties have an essential role to play which may otherwise go by default.

There are, of course, a large variety of voluntary organisations, some of them are explicitly or implicitly clubs of upper and middle class or sectarian interests (including many of the Residents' Welfare Associations in metropolitan cities, and dominant caste associations in rural areas). In this essay, I shall largely confine myself to those organisations which are dedicated to the cause of the poor or the victims of human rights abuse. Even among the latter I shall exclude some of the organisations clearly affiliated to different political parties (like the major trade unions and some women's organisations). [I shall mostly avoid the widely-used term, the nongovernmental organisation or NGO, as the latter encompasses too many diverse types of organisations (after all, Al Qaida is among the most well-known NGOs in the world today), and in India some of the NGO interests represented in the National Advisory Council (NAC) presided over by the Congress President are in some sense a more important part of the Government of India than many of the administrative departments in Delhi.]

ACHIEVEMENTS

The voluntary sector activists in India have much to be proud of: landmark laws like the Right to Information Act, frequent calling of attention to human rights abuses, torture of prisoners, and police and army atrocities in different parts of India, the National Rural Employment Guarantee Act, associations to help self-employed workers and to monitor and coordinate community health and education services, forest rights for *adivasis*, mid-day meals for schoolchildren, and so on. Under their leadership the environmental movement against forest degradation, water and air pollution, and the like has been active, particularly in consciousness-raising on such vital issues. In a country where people easily despair of their government, these activists have shown that vigilance and struggles do yield some results in goading governments (including courts) to act, though often very slowly.

Even though no common ideology unites the various pro-poor groups in the voluntary sector, many are inspired by Gandhian or leftist or "green" (conservationist) ideas. On the three major coordination mechanisms in society—the state, market, and the community—they are usually anti-market, and sometimes anti-state, and almost invariably in favour of community-level organisations. Like most small-is-beautiful communitarians, they often underplay the tyrannies of local communities in day-to-day life (even outside the dispensations of *khap panchayats*) and the ease with which local organisations are often captured by the elite and the powerful. It is also important to remember that Ambedkar, unlike Gandhi, had more trust in larger representative institutions and laws, away from the "cesspool" of village society. In economic matters, the small-scale of production in some lines of activity severely inhibits economies of scale and technological upgrading, and investment in high-return high-risk projects (which require risk-pooling with larger non-local entities), and this is ultimately inequitable as it keeps those small producers mired in low productivity and stagnation, as the large part of the vast informal sector in India is.

AGAINST THE MARKET

The social activists are often united with the traditional Left parties in opposing market liberalisation. They undervalue the important disciplining and coordinating functions of the market, and unwittingly strengthen the hands of politicians and bureaucrats who want to preserve their control over state monopoly, patronage distribution and corrupt income. Socially also the anonymity of the market may have liberating effects for the social downtrodden, as some *dalit* intellectuals have pointed out. How much of the unleashing of entrepreneurial energies in the last three decades of gradual market liberalisation and relatively high economic growth that economists usually refer to is linked up with the effects of the concomitant political rise of the hitherto subordinate social groups in roughly the same decades is an under-researched area in Indian economic sociology.

SINGLE-INTEREST LOBBIES

The social activists, even while drawing upon Gandhian "enlightened anarchism" (of *Hind Swaraj*) or the postmodernist critiques of the modernising state for their ideological sustenance, do not usually hesitate to turn to the state (including the judiciary) for relief and protection of the small people against large producers and developers, venal officials and marauding communal groups. In the government policy arena they often act as self-appointed lobbies for the poor and the oppressed. While this lobbying activity is at least as legitimate as that by trade unions, farmers' associations or chambers of commerce, one should keep in mind that such non-party organisations cannot and should not replace the role of traditional party organisations, however, much the latter are associated with corrupt politics in the eyes of activists. Voluntary groups, as single-interest advocacy lobbies, inherently lack the mechanism of transactional negotiations and give-and-take among diverse interest groups that large party organisations representing and encompassing those diverse interests could (and used to) facilitate.

COMPLEX TRADE-OFFS

This kind of give-and-take is particularly important when many controversial issues of the day—large dams, land acquisition, extraction of minerals in tribal areas, habitat-displacing development projects—involve complex trade-offs and balancing of diverse interests which single-interest lobby groups necessarily slur over. Even those who speak in the name of the poor usually under-stress the diversity among the poor—a dam may benefit thousands of small farmers in hitherto dry land, while displacing thousands of others, a development project may displace some from ancestral land but provide jobs and new and more productive livelihoods for others, and so on. Each such case involves complex trade-offs and the need for negotiated compromises and compensations, both across groups and over time (short run vs long run). It is possible that after careful balancing of the gains and losses one may still conclude that the dam should not be constructed or the development project should not be undertaken. But this should be the outcome of a deliberative process within a party forum where diverse interests and stakeholders are represented, rather than a reaction simply to the shrillness and agitational or financial resources of any particular single-interest lobby. Of course, such deliberative processes are not always encouraged within the existing political parties, either because of the compulsions of raising election funds from vested interests or because most of the major political parties in India today have no inner-party democracy, with issues and leaders even at the local level decided from above. But this is more a matter of restoring democracy within party organisations, instead of giving in to single-interest lobbies, however, pious the intentions of the latter may be.

This is where the forum of Left parties has an important role to play, even though they have largely abdicated it, except in occasional rhetoric. If they can play an active role in organising the vast numbers of informal sector workers (the modes of organising them are quite different from those in the formal sector, as I indicated in my earlier article in *Economic & Political Weekly* referred to at the beginning), then along with their current strength among workers in the formal sector they can provide a substantial countervailing power to the corporate oligarchy and corrupt politicians that dominate the Indian polity. As Left parties they should be more attuned to the debates on the historical role of capitalism (vis-à-vis forces of pre-capitalism). As Joan Robinson once said, what is worse than being "exploited" is not to be "exploited" at all.

While being sensitive to the struggles of the poor, the Left parties, compared to some activist groups, are also more aware of the value Marx placed on technological progress and development of the "forces of production", even when the latter inevitably cause community-wrenching displacement.

Some of the conflicting interests among the poor and the trade-offs can be sorted out within the party if the deliberative process is transparent and accountable, which in Leninist parties is currently blocked by the repressive bludgeon of "democratic centralism".

Of all the social scientists, economists, by the nature of their disciplinary training, spend a great deal of their professional time and skills on thinking about complex trade-offs and appropriate methods of empirically evaluating the comparative costs and benefits which vary from case to case. While some of them may be "sold out" to vested interests, many of them are sincere in their on-the-one-hand, on-the-other hand arguments when it comes to policy debates. It is not a coincidence that many single-interest social activist groups (who in their mind already know where truth lies) are irritated by such modes of open-minded argument and methods of experimental evaluation employed by economists. (In the current debates on the food security policy, for example, NAC and associated activists are vehemently opposed to some economists' suggestions about trying out alternative cash-based transfers at least as pilot experiments in parts of the country in place of the highly wasteful and corrupt public distribution system. In general, in policy debates they show much less concern for the colossal inefficiencies of government spending programmes.) Ardent belief or missionary zeal in a cause can sometimes be dismissive of complexity, and make one prone to think that those who argue for the need for scepticism and trial and error must be enemies to the cause. The same, of course, is the case with some market-fundamentalist or orthodox-Left economists.

PREOCCUPATION WITH REDISTRIBUTION

The social activists share with the Left parties a preoccupation with issues of redistribution, and they often resort to nothing more than hand-waving when it comes to complex issues of ensuring the sustained generation of a large enough surplus out of which the redistribution is to be done. Faced with those issues the Left usually refers to the great things the State can do, and the social activists will refer you to the great things small producers and community-based organisations can do. There are not too many systemic, large-scale, viable and incentive-compatible examples of these around to instil confidence in a sceptic's mind. In their absence, the social activists as well as the Left are now mainly associated with populist causes, which in the long run are often wasteful and counterproductive.

LIMITS OF RIGHTS-BASED APPROACH

While the Left emphasises worker rights, the social activists emphasise citizen's rights (to food, education, information, jobs on public works, etc). The latter are more relevant to many informal workers. The activists' rights-based approach has a lot to commend: it serves to raise consciousness among the poor and vulnerable informal workers about their entitlements to social protection, a sense that they are not mere supplicants to the politicians and bureaucrats. But one should not ignore the limitations of this approach. If the delivery structure for implementing some of these rights remains as weak and corrupt as it is now, mere promulgation of rights will remain hollow and will, after a point, generate only cynicism. The Indian public arena is already littered with hundreds of unenforced or spasmodically enforced court injunctions, some of them on the implementation of rights, and there is some danger that the proliferating judicial activism, egged on by the rights-based movement and the media, may end up, for all the good intentions, in undermining the credibility and legitimacy of the judiciary itself.

Finally, while our politicians and their hypocrisy and criminality often provide an unedifying spectacle, some civil society groups or unelected entities sympathetic with their cause, by their constant implicit or explicit disparagement of the institutions of representative government, unwittingly weaken the democratic process. In the history of Africa, Latin America, and in other parts of South Asia, the widespread disparagement of representative institutions has made it easier for populist authoritarianism to get a grip and entrench itself. The politicians are at least subject to periodic electoral accountability, while their critics are the depository of all the right answers and largely unaccountable (or accountable only to the donors in the case of well-funded organisations). As it is, our influential middle classes who are often too impatient with the slow and dirty processes through which the numerical majority of the unwashed and the uneducated give their democratic verdict, are always on the lookout for short cuts to cleaner politics, national prestige and superpower status. They latch on to holy men that our civil society throws up from time to time, sanctimoniously offering us magic potions in Gandhi caps or red robes, cheered on by the sensation-seeking electronic media. Some of our holier-than thou *jholawalas* who already know all the answers to complex questions are in some danger of joining that ragtag army of self-proclaimed do-gooders.

At the same time let me hasten to add that one should not detract the value of the large numbers of grass roots social workers India is fortunate to have, who spend less time on discrediting the political process and concentrate more on working at the local level for the cause of the deprived. They also work on increasing people's awareness and information, catalysing their organisations in demanding the delivery of social services, participating in serious field experiments to find out the best ways of devising the delivery mechanisms, and acting as watchdogs against the abuses of state and corporate power—thereby immeasurably strengthening the democratic process.

CHAPTER 8

An Interview with *The Telegraph*

30 December 2013

POLITICS OF DOLE

Business people use this expression—politics of dole—to describe money spent on anti-poverty programmes and I have objections to this term. Most of the subsidies of the Indian government are actually to the business class and middle and upper classes, but that is not regarded as dole. Giving help to the poor for education, health, food or employment is called dole and to me, this is really tendentious. This serves to distract from the huge amount of subsidies and handouts of the government to better-off people in the form of petroleum subsidies, diesel, fertiliser, LPG and several other subsidies. There are estimates that suggest that the amount of subsidies for better-off people is about three to four times more than the money the government spends on anti-poverty programmes.

Secondly, I am not sure the recent Assembly election results proved that giving help to the poor does not work. Both in Madhya Pradesh and Chhattisgarh, the incumbent government won and they had some successful anti-poverty programmes (including, for example, employment and food security programmes). It so happens that in Rajasthan, where the

Congress government focused on some measures for the poor, it did not succeed electorally . . . One does not know whether (Ashok) Gehlot lost just because he was depending on anti-poverty programmes, some people say that his party has been undermined by internal faction fights.

Thirdly, some of these programmes are not always helping the poor. If they are effectively delivered, not just the poor people benefit, the entire economy benefits at least through productivity rise. So, one should not look upon them only as unproductive doles. The problem is, the way they are delivered in most parts of India, there is a lot of leakage and inefficiency. One should try to stop those.

But this is not an argument that effective service delivery to the poor will be enough for bringing about economic growth, you also need to build infrastructure—roads, electricity and ports.

SEN VERSUS BHAGWATI

The media turned an honest debate into a political football and misinterpreted the intentions of both sides. I have seen statements in the media that (Amartya) Sen and (Jean) Dreze are providing the rationale for Congress policies, whereas (Jagdish) Bhagwati and (Arvind) Panagariya are providing that for Modi or the BJP. One should not forget that Sen and Dreze are often very critical of the Congress party. Also, Bhagwati has said some good things about Modi, but he does not support everything about him.

Let me say that people are underestimating the similarities in their positions on the policy issue and distorting their genuine differences. The similarities are, as I understand it, both sides want reforms, both sides want growth and both sides want reduction in poverty. On these three things, both sides agree.

The difference is in terms of the methods of achieving those objectives. Bhagwati, as I understand it, says you cannot on a sustainable basis help the poor unless you focus on growth. It is the growth that will bring down poverty that is the argument. Directly, growth provides more jobs to the poor. Secondly, once growth happens, it generates more tax revenues and there will be more to spend on the poor.

I think these are generally correct propositions. But while the first proposition is theoretically correct, it so happens that in India growth has not created that many jobs. The economy has grown at a fast rate between 2003 and 2008-09, but not enough jobs have been created. Even Gujarat's high industrial growth in recent years has largely involved expansion of the petro-chemical sector, which is highly capital-intensive.

Bhagwati and his associates have sometimes said that growth has not created enough employment in India because of bureaucratic controls, particularly labour regulations. I personally think that while labour laws may put some restrictions, it is not the main reason why employment is not growing. For employment growth, we also need basic infrastructure—electricity, roads—and adequate vocational training and skill formation among workers.

The second proposition is also right that growth will result in more revenues and you can spend the extra revenue on poor people. But there is no guarantee that just because the government has extra money, they will spend it on poor people.

In a sense, Dreze and Sen are trying to create public awareness of the importance of using this extra revenue for the poor. If nobody demands it, nobody protests about it, much of the handouts will go as they have always gone to the better off. So the Bhagwati position, even when correct, may not be enough to transform the lives of the poor. You may need to have specific policies and provisions of helping the poor, otherwise poverty will not automatically decline at a fast enough pace. I largely agree with Sen and Dreze. But some people have got the impression that their view is that growth is important, but if you do more on health, education and nutrition that will provide more growth because people will be more productive.

I think as I have already mentioned that itself may not be enough (as the experience of Maoist China or Kerala and Sri Lanka in the recent past shows). You need particularly better infrastructure—like electricity and roads—and a better investment climate, for which you may need less controls, regulations and bureaucratic delays. It is also the case that just pushing more money into anti-poverty programmes is not enough, the delivery structure and governance need a major overhaul. But Dreze and Sen point out some remarkable improvements in a few states in recent years in this matter.

INDIA CATCHING UP WITH CHINA

These are the two largest countries of the world, with ancient agrarian civilisations, and with the adoption of sharply different political and economic regimes, and so they are often compared. Around 1990, per capita income was very similar between the two countries. Since 1990, China has grown at a much faster rate and also removed poverty at a much faster rate than India. Now the question is often asked, will they converge? On that question, the point is: converge in what?

I think most people have in mind converging in terms of the growth rate. There are reasons to think that the Chinese growth rate will go down, say in the next 15 years. One, because the Chinese population is ageing faster whereas India is a much younger country. Younger people are more productive than old people. So, on that ground alone, some people think that India's growth is going to go up and Chinese growth is going to go down because of this demographic advantage for India.

I should qualify this; India's demographic advantage is only a potential advantage. Now, the question is whether that potential will be realised. Yes, there will be a lot of young people. But for them to contribute to the economy, you have to give them good jobs. Unfortunately, fertility rates being what they are in different parts of India, this bulge of young people will be in less well-governed states like Bihar, Uttar Pradesh—where fertility rates are high—but not in the south, where the fertility rates have already gone down quite a bit. So, if this large number of young people in different parts of north India does not get good jobs, it might be politically explosive as there will be a huge number of unemployed people.

There is another argument that over time the Chinese savings rate will go down and to that extent the help that economic growth gets from savings will not be there. The third reason is in order to grow faster, the Chinese will need new innovations. As of now, there is no comparison between innovations in the US, Japan, Germany and China. India, of course, is innovating less than China.

Though the Chinese are trying in a big way through investments in research and development, and they are expected to do better than us, one does not know how far they will be able to compensate for the other reasons why growth will go down.

Right now, India is growing at 4 to 5 per cent and I do not see any reason why India cannot grow at 7 to 8 per cent. So, the Chinese growth rate is likely to fall in the next 15 years, while India's average long run growth rate will be higher than today's level and so they will come nearer.

Mere convergence of growth rates does not, however, mean that the gap in levels of living in the two countries will converge. Even if their growth rates are the same, the gaps in levels of living will still remain. For this gap to be bridged, India has to grow at a substantially faster rate than China, but that does not look realistic.

CONCERN ABOUT INDIA'S REFORM AGENDA

I am not very happy with the focus on the financial sector liberalisation for the last few years. I am largely in favour of liberalisation in the rest of the economy—agriculture, industry, trade—but finance is something different. If you liberalise the financial sector too much, the money can rush out of the country quickly and that can have very bad effect on the economy. Some Latin American countries have suffered from this for quite some time.

In the matter of financial sector liberalisation, India has, for many years, maintained caution. But for the last two to three years, it seems that caution is going down. For example, the macro managers are allowing large short-term dollar denominated debts, which I think can be very dangerous. Many economies have suffered when their short-term dollar denominated debts have gone out of control. On the issue of short-term debt, capital flows and financial sector liberalisation, I think there should be much more careful and extensive debate in the country.

CHANGE IN BENGAL

I have not seen substantial change either in industrial expansion or in investment in infrastructure. I also do not see any substantial change in skill formation. I think the issue of land acquisition, on which the earlier government had problems in the context of industrial expansion, is yet to be resolved. Though it seems some sense is dawning on the new government that the problem has to be addressed. The new Land Acquisition Act that the central government has adopted is flawed in many respects, but it is a step in the right direction.

Apart from land, one needs capital. In Bengal, local capital and entrepreneurial spirit are not that strong. The business sector has not been healthy for quite some time, the state has a lot of declining industries, and the declining industries have not been replaced by new thriving industries. So, there is a long way to go. Land is one constraint, capital is another and infrastructure is another constraint.

What Bengal needs now is a sensible discussion and a concerted approach by all. There are many intelligent people in all political parties in Bengal. Besides, there are people who are not political people at all. Let us all sit down together and thrash out the issues.

Unfortunately, the situation in Bengal for a long time is highly politically polarised and that is not helping a sensible discussion. This political polarisation has been a major problem in Bengal. Now, Trinamool has won the elections both at the state and panchayat levels, but one has to see whether they will be able to give leadership in new directions.

TAKING THE MIDDLE PATH

I do not really believe that Left and Right labels mean much. I think one has to be clear about one's objectives. I would consider myself Left if by Left people mean a commitment to social justice. But if the meaning of Left implies necessarily favouring the state over markets, I am not Left.

I personally think that the market has a lot to contribute in coordination of resource allocation and disciplining inefficiency. If you do not allow market competition, then the state tends to be a monopoly and that might be exploiting the poor as much as a private monopoly. So, the market to me— particularly in the sense of active competition—is important. As soon as you hear this, you may say this person is not Left. This is the wrong way to look about it.

Most of us want social justice. But the question is, how do you get there? What are the issues?

There comes the importance of the middle way. I will say both the state's and market's roles are important. In that sense, I am in favour of both, and eager to curb the excesses and distortions of both. A large part of the world is realising this. Take for example the case of China. China is a so-called communist country, but China has gone for capitalism and for market in a much bigger way than India. This is a peculiar situation today, that the most vigorous pursuit of capitalism in the world today is being presided over by a party which calls itself communist. That means, in reality if not in rhetoric, they are taking a middle way, too. They know that the state has a big role, but they are giving tremendous importance to the market.

It is an example that the most successful way is to take the middle path.

ACHIEVING ACADEMIC EXCELLENCE

In India, the education bureaucracy interferes and stifles in every sphere of education—from student admission, curriculum development, rigid examination systems to faculty appointment, promotions and salaries, and research grants.

My support is more for autonomy and avoidance of political interference, if one's goal is achieving academic excellence.

Total independence, however, to the institution may have its own problems. This might create a low-level equilibrium of mediocrity and cronyism. The good American universities escape this through a culture of competition, and good teachers move to another university if they are dissatisfied with the low-level equilibrium of mediocrity, and that is true for good students as well.

The mediocrity of education levels in West Bengal has pushed many good students (and faculty) to go elsewhere. But competition also causes problems and markets often lead to inequality. Say a student from a humble background in Purulia may not be as mobile as students from better-off backgrounds. The way to solve this problem is by providing generous scholarships and student loans, so that everyone gets a chance to be mobile.

So, instead of interfering with the affairs of academic institutions, the politicians and bureaucrats should try to create an atmosphere of competition in which even the poorest student gets an opportunity. But this is a time-consuming process.

CHAPTER 9

An Interview with *The Indian Express*

5 March 2014

Q: Issues of growth and welfare are likely to come up again in the election campaign. The Sen-Bhagwati argument was a marker of the debate. Is it really about welfare versus growth?

A: People like Bhagwati believe we should concentrate on economic growth and the poor will ultimately be helped; whereas, if you concentrate on other things, growth might suffer and as a result, so will the poor. In that chain of arguments, there is a dual process. One is that high growth means more jobs. So if the poor have more jobs, they will have more income. Two, if there is growth, the economy expands and taxes go up.

With that money, you can fund anti-poverty programmes. On the face of it, this is a plausible argument. But it does not always work. For instance, even in the highest growth period in India, say between 2003-08, most of the evidence shows that employment did not grow much. Now, from a poor person's perspective, what is the point of growth if you cannot get a job? For example, the highly cited Gujarat model claims a high rate of growth, but employment grew only marginally. That is the general trend: high growth does not necessarily lead to higher employment. Bhagwati's first channel needs to be shown to be working. If you look at the employment data, the only industry in India that created significant jobs in the high growth period is the construction industry. Let me not go here into the issue why employment grows so sluggishly in India.

Regarding the indirect channel, my objection is that it is not automatic. Most of the data show that in India, much of the revenue goes towards subsidies. Analysis shows that the overwhelming proportion of subsidies in India goes to the relatively better off, the rich, the corporate sector and the middle class. So it is not necessarily true that just because the government gets more money, it will spend on the poor. Again, let us look at Modi's Gujarat government. Under Modi's tenure, I saw data that the total amount of subsidies to the corporate sector, especially in the form of tax concessions and capital subsidies, was 10 times more than what was spent on subsidies to agriculture and food subsidies etc.

In that context, people like Sen say that since it is not automatic that the money coming to the government is spent on the poor, we have to shout for it. In my judgement, they are trying to give strength to the voices of the poor, so that more money is spent on them. The problem is that even if they succeed in getting the government to spend more money, it may not always reach the poor. So there comes the question of delivery mechanisms. Sen and Dreze should emphasise this more. Also, they give the impression that all you need to do for growth is to spend more money on health, education and nutrition, and that will make people more productive, which will lead to growth. I think that yes, when workers are healthier and better educated they will be more productive. But that is not enough. Even when you have a productive workforce, you need other things, like physical infrastructure and a good investment climate. Private investors need the right incentive to invest. Just having a productive workforce is not enough, and one has to pay attention to some of the reform issues emphasised by Bhagwati.

Q: Given all the talk of the Gujarat model, how would you rate Modi's governance record?

A: Modi has tried to make governance his main election plank, because he thinks he has a good record. He has done some good things, like electricity reform, which has gone quite far in Gujarat. He has also done well in taking quick decisions and he completely controls the government. But that would not translate at the Centre; governing this vast, complex, heterogeneous country is very different. His style is to steamroll over opposition, but at the national level this would be a major problem. His personality is polarising and he creates controversy, rather than building consensus. Even if this works in Gujarat, on a pan-India level, he will have serious problems.

In terms of political governance, 2002 was a disastrous governance failure. Modi will of course say that the SIT has given him a clean chit. There are problems with this position, but even ignoring those, he cannot deny that something horrible happened under his watch. The responsibility is on you, particularly when you control the government with so firm a hand. Your own people have now been indicted. If a politician looks the other way or subcontracts the job of communalism to others, it is a sign of extremely bad governance. Vajpayee spoke of Modi deviating from *rajdharma*. Someone rebuked by his own prime minister for a lapse in *rajdharma* cannot go around thumping his "56-inch chest" on governance.

On economic governance, Modi has many achievements. But at the same time one has to recognise that he has given a lot of subsidies to the corporate sector. Modi may be business-friendly, but he is not necessarily market-friendly. One should distinguish between the two. If you embrace subsidies, you cannot then complain about welfare programmes for the poor. You are giving doles to the corporate sector, which deserve it much less. In manufacturing, Gujarat's rank among Indian states was No. 2 thirty years back, and it has remained No. 2 under Modi. Much of the industrial growth under Modi has been in petroleum refineries which create very few jobs. Gujarat's delivery mechanism for public services is not particularly notable. It is not bad, but other states have done much better. In general, Tamil Nadu and Himachal Pradesh have performed much better than Gujarat. If you compare the 2001 and 2011 Census figures on literacy, Gujarat's rank among the states actually declined. Modi's trumpeting of himself as *Vikaspurush* cannot hide the fact that in overall economic performance (counting both growth and welfare services) quite a few other states have performed much better.

Q: Decentralisation is an idea that has gained prominence with the rise of the Aam Aadmi Party. What are your views?
A: It is good that Arvind Kejriwal is in favour of decentralisation. However, I find in him an insufficient appreciation of the problems of decentralisation. He thinks *mohalla sabhas* are going to do everything, but *mohalla sabhas* in large parts of Delhi would be mostly RWAs, which are middle class, not *aam aadmi*. I have worked on decentralisation for the last 15-20 years, and most of my village survey work is in West Bengal. Decentralisation has partly worked there, but there are still big problems. There is collusion between local politicians and other vested interests. They essentially capture the panchayat, maybe less in Bengal than in UP, where the *sarpanch* is essentially in the pocket of the local politician and landed interests. Even in West Bengal there is a lot of political clientelism. Capture is a big problem. It is much easier to capture a panchayat than the Lok Sabha. One of the reasons why decentralisation has not worked in India is because we have not really embraced the idea. We passed 73rd and 74th Constitutional Amendments but did not follow

through at the level of the State governments. So, even if you have a good panchayat, you do not have the money. The money is coming from above, and that is where the power is. Even if the panchayat is not captured, it would not succeed unless it has more autonomy and power. The other issue is that it is not enough to have money. Quite often, in villages, there is no expertise. A lot of corruption takes place because there simply is not the capability to do book-keeping or auditing. Ultimately it is a matter of money because if there was a lot of money, expertise could be hired. But funds from panchayat budgets go unspent because viable projects are not undertaken or completed due to a lack of expertise.

Q: Corruption has emerged as an election issue and we have seen the Aam Aadmi Party form a government on that plank. How effective do you think something like the Lokpal is?

A: Kejriwal and his party should be lauded for bringing the issue in the open, but they do not seem to have thought it through. They always talk of punishing the bribe-taker. The lokpal they want may be effective in punishing the official. What about the much wealthier bribe-giver? To me, that is just, as if, not more important. There are also some institutional issues here. One, there has to be institutional change so that the bribe-giver does not have the incentive to give bribes. Two, this assumes that all the corruption is official corruption. But a large part of corruption in India is within the private sector. Lokpal cannot do anything about that. Three, they have not thought enough about why there is corruption. You are a powerful public official and I have to go to you as a supplicant for a death or marriage or caste certificate, etc. I have to please you, so I pay a bribe. You have the power because you are the only person who can give me the certificate. What if there were a hundred other people who could also give me the certificate? Then there would be competition and bribery would decline. For example, in India you have a lot of corruption in the passport office. You do not see that in the US, but it is not because they are more moral than us. There you go to the nearby post office and apply for the passport. Suppose the postal officer asks for a bribe, you go to another post office. You deprive the postal officer of the monopoly power over passport applications. Much official corruption occurs because of monopoly power. Many supporters of AAP think corruption is just a matter of personal morals or insufficient punishment. China has the severest punishment for corruption (sometimes, execution), yet corruption is rampant there. Even if I assume everyone is immoral, dishonest, there are ways of reducing corruption by changing the institutional rules to create competition. One needs to come up with institutional changes that could reduce the incentive to give a bribe. The Aam Aadmi Party's approach so far has been rather naive.

Q: Do you think *Aadhaar* can address corruption?
A: I am generally in favour of *Aadhaar*, though I understand that there are some concerns people have raised about privacy. But I think the potential benefits from *Aadhaar* outweigh some of these. But I do not think we should expect too much from it. Some types of corruption problems will be solved, but others will not. For instance, for the food security bill, or NREGA, *Aadhaar* will solve the problem of fake job cards or faked identities. So if your biometric data do not match, it can address that. But it cannot solve the problem of faked BPL cards, for instance. Because, BPL is means-tested, *Aadhaar* is not. Some of the corruption will remain, like the non-poor grabbing the resources meant for the poor, because *Aadhaar* cannot weigh the definition of the poor. People should have realistic expectations. A good thing is that it is portable, where migrant workers will be now able to access services,

or pavement dwellers with no fixed address can get, say, ration cards. However, there are legal issues, like whether it is voluntary or not. If it is voluntary, then it might not be as useful. What has started worrying me in the last 3-4 weeks is that the Congress party seems to be backtracking on its own big project. It is particularly wrong sign when you start with big fanfare and then backtrack—at least that is the impression.

Q: Are the civil services to blame for the gaps in delivery?

A: In the civil services, the system creates warped incentives. There are risks to taking a bold decision. It may or may not work. When I know that vigilance offices are always watching me, I would not take a bold decision. Why? Because if I do, and it does not work, and somebody gains as a result of the decision not working, then there will be an ostensible case, as if I took the decision deliberately to profit that man. Whereas if I take the non-risky but low-payoff decision, the company does not gain much, but I save my skin, which one will I take? This obsession with affixing blame is part of the problem of why, say, public sector enterprises are inefficient. We do not incentivise bureaucrats to make bold decisions. This is in contrast to China, where the local official's promotion depends on certain well-specified criteria. One is the economic performance of the district you are in charge of. Suppose, I am a corrupt local official, I will still steal, but not too much, because if I do that then my district's performance suffers. And I would not get promoted. So it is in my self-interest to ensure the district does well. Indian district collectors have no such incentive. If the district goes to the dogs, it does not matter, s/he will be transferred in two years anyway. The Chinese system is non-democratic but they think in terms of incentives, we are not.

Q: You mentioned earlier that there are no jobs being created. But the jobs that are created go unfilled because of skills deficit. How can that be addressed?

A: For me, the skill-formation question is a major issue, one that goes to the much larger issue of how to restructure the education system. No government seems to have given enough thought to this. They announce more universities, more IITs and IIMs, but that is not the way to address this very real problem. I have suggested that we borrow ideas from Germany and the US. In Germany, after you leave school or even Grade 8, this whole population is streamed towards vocational training, acquiring specialised skills. These vocational training centres collaborate with firms that are potential employers, who also fund them. By getting involved in vocational training, they can catch good workers early, so these students are like trainees in the company. That is a model that is highly imitable in India. In the US, the overwhelming majority of high school graduates go to community colleges, which are local. They are funded entirely by local taxes, are almost free and extremely accessible. The tiny percentage of people who do very well can transfer to universities. That is how it should be. How many people are really cut out for good university education? Most people go into jobs for which you do not need a bachelors or a masters degree. We need to adapt these models to our circumstances and restructure our education system to encourage skill formation. It is also important to link up to potential job-givers and involve them in the process. We should be setting up skills-training centres in villages and small towns, rather than expanding universities.

Q: There have been reports that growth rates in China are coming down and that we do not know what is going on there.

A: There is no doubt that China's growth rates are slowing. For one, it is ageing. I expect the growth rate to decline over time, but not that much, because its savings rate is very high, and with that kind of savings rate, you cannot do too badly. Indeed the reason I think India's growth rate will also rebound is that the savings rate is reasonably high. The other reason for China's growth rate to remain high is that they are spending a large part of the GDP on R&D, which will lead to innovation and growth. China is already beating the US on green technology, and they are looking for sectors they can enter.

Q: There is a perception that we cannot trust Chinese data.
A: That is true but there are indirect ways of checking on industrial growth, like electricity consumption etc. So those checks largely show that there is only a little gap between official statistics and independent estimates. Either way, Chinese growth rate is very high. Having said that, India's service sector growth is very badly recorded and India's data are only slightly better than Chinese data.

Q: But the sense is that the poor quality of Indian data are due to incompetence, while Chinese data are political.
A: Sure. But Indian data can also be political. State government may change their data because of the criteria of fund allocation. So I would not be surprised if there were corresponding manipulations in Indian data also. No doubt it is much more in China though. I expect that by 2020, their growth rate will come down to 6-7 per cent.

Q: Do you think a lower growth rate will stress the political system and force the Communist Party to make political concessions?
A: Well, 6-7 per cent is not all that low. I think the political unrest will come from other reasons. As a result of growth, property prices have gone up, and therefore, even the middle class cannot afford houses. That is a source of resentment. Secondly, eventually the middle class will start questioning the government's actions, as is already happening on micro-blogs. But it is difficult to predict. The government knows socialism does not hold the country together. It is trying to substitute—the glue now is

nationalism. Every Chinese learns in school of a century of humiliation—that 19th century on, from the Opium War, they have been humiliated. And now is the time to reclaim their position in the world. So they have cleverly used nationalism. I would not be surprised if things explode, but if I were to bet, the Party will probably manage to control things for some time to come.

CHAPTER 10

An Interview with *Business Standard*

16 December 2011

Q: The Indian economy seems to be in turmoil, with industrial growth contracting 5.1 per cent in October 2011 and the fiscal deficit running high. What are the options before the government?

A: Let us look at the recent reform in retail that has been held up. I am in favour of opening the retail sector. It is not just about foreign investment but also about reforming domestic retail. There are two kinds of opposition. One is that small kirana stores will suffer and the other is the "East India Company syndrome", where foreigners will exploit our farmers. Both are misguided. They say foreigners will come and exploit our farmers. What is happening now? Our own traders are exploiting the farmers today. In most states, the food ministry decides on a small number of traders who will buy from farmers. This gives traders monopoly power. So there is collusion. The food ministries in most states are highly corrupt. They get money from traders and select two or three of them; these traders get monopoly powers and exploit farmers.

Q: So you mean the entry of foreign companies will ensure that traders lose that monopoly power?

A: The way to reduce exploitation is to increase competition from whichever source. So if Walmart or Carrefour want to buy from farmers, they should be allowed to do so. That way, if someone is paying a farmer low prices, he can sell his produce to someone else. So the important thing is competition. FDI is also advantageous since foreign players have a lot of money to invest in cold storage. At least 40 to 50 per cent of our fruit and vegetables go waste for lack of cold storage and refrigerated transport. This requires high initial investment. There is no reason Reliance cannot do this, the distinction between foreign and domestic retail does not matter. But foreign retailers can also bring technology in inventory management, which is very important.

Q: But do you believe that kirana stores will bear the brunt at the cost of increased technology, back-end infrastructure and reforms?

A: Any small kirana shop near a big Reliance shop will suffer. But there are ways to avoid that. Quite often, small shops do not get their supply from farmers but buy from monopoly traders. On allowing foreign retailers, these small stores may buy from foreign retailers. These large operations will have economies of scale. And kirana stores will now get supplies at a cheaper price. So they will benefit.

Another reason kirana shops will not go out of business is that, quite often, poor people buy on credit and not cash. Also, in many big shops, you pay through credit cards; since poor people do not have credit cards, they will go to kirana shops.

Finally, in many remote tribal areas, big shops would not work. No one will travel 100 km to buy. So corner shops have to be there. Do not expect them to be wiped out. They will have some competition in big cities, but will also have advantages, as they will buy cheap.

Also, the big retail chains can use small shops as local agents of big stores. Think about these things. Otherwise, the discussion is oversimplified. I do not think either party is thinking properly on the issue.

Q: India's economic growth today is being supported mainly by services, which do not create as many jobs as manufacturing. Growth in industry or manufacturing is on the decline. How do you see this?

A: Service is a huge sector. We think a major part of services comes from software, real estate, finance and so on. But all of this together will not even constitute one-third of the services sector. So, it depends on which service sector we are talking about. We have not seen much data about how the informal sector is linked to the formal sector. One kind of informal sector supplies to the formal sector. So, if the formal sector develops, the informal sector will also develop. Of course, we cannot generalise but some parts of the informal service sector are also expanding. For example, private tuition is an informal service that is growing fast. The religious tourism sector is also expanding. In some parts of the services sector, the only way to resolve the problem is to provide better social transfers, better electricity.

Q: There is a big debate on subsidies and whether the government should curtail them. How do you see that?

A: Our country grows by nine or 10 per cent, yet half of our population does not share in this growth. It is unsustainable growth, which is not legitimate. But spending or throwing money at something is not enough; the real problem is that more than half of social spending is wasted or stolen. The government should spend more on health, education, vocational training, public sanitation and so on. Essentially, the government should redesign the spending structure first, and then reform it. It is not just a fiscal issue, but a political issue.

Q: There is a huge debate over the Food Security Bill in India. The Cabinet deferred the issue this week owing to differences over the subsidy burden. What do you think?

A: Coming to the Food Security Bill, it is not just a question of fiscal consolidation. Yes, social sector spending is very high, but we need to think about how much subsidy goes to the relatively rich. Nearly two-thirds of the subsidy goes to the relatively rich, which is about nine per cent of GDP. If we are giving nine per cent to the relatively rich, we should not mind giving one or two per cent to the poor. Now, if the food security Bill is implemented, it will account for nearly one per cent of the budget. Nobody talks of the nine per cent that goes to the rich. What is needed is realignment as well as reallocation of resources.

Q: And how do we do that?

A: For instance, if you take the diesel subsidy, much of it goes into expensive cars and a large part of the subsidy on kerosene is used in trucks, while more than half the utilisation of LPG cooking gas is by the middle and upper classes, not the poor. We have a subsidy on higher education, when most poor people drop out at primary and middle levels. So we need to reallocate subsidies. It does not necessarily involve increasing total spending but needs realignment.

CHAPTER 11

An Economist's View
on the New Government's Initiatives

Ideas for India, 19 December 2014

Q: What do you make of the policies of the new Indian government so far? Do you see more continuity or change?

A: As in most things, I see both continuity and change. In fact, some of the announcements that have been made are continuation to earlier policies. The *Swachh Bharat Abhiyan*, announced with much fanfare and broom-wielding by politicians stepping out of their limousines for photo-op, for instance, is largely the same as the *Nirmal Bharat Abhiyan*, the earlier government had launched. This government has probably more energy and will probably do more, but one has to understand issues such as why toilets built in the earlier programme did not get used. One obvious reason is the absence of regular water supply to keep toilets usable. Even without that problem, there are several social and cultural issues that come up, which cannot be solved merely by bureaucratic fiat.

For instance, why is it that the toilet programme has succeeded much more in Bangladesh, a poorer country, than in India? One does not really know, but a part of the answer may be that as in other social programmes in Bangladesh these are not just *sarkari* (government) programmes foisted from above. Non-government organisations (NGOs) got involved in working with the common people on these projects, particularly in changing habits of personal hygiene. Another answer that has been given by some—and which we should discuss and find out more about—is that Hindu culture instils some deep aversion to cleaning toilets. For centuries, our toilets have been cleaned by people who have occupied the lowest and most degraded rungs of the social hierarchy.

So, even if you give people toilets but they are not willing to clean them, they will often remain unused. This is less true of primarily non-Hindu societies like Bangladesh. The new government's energy to solve this issue is welcome but they must understand (and that is where the continuity part comes in) why the earlier programme did not work.

Similarly, one programme that the government has announced, and which I am generally in favour of, is the *Jan Dhan Yojana*. But here, too, the government must understand why more than 40 per cent of households have so far lacked banking access. It is difficult to reach out to remote areas of the country. The idea of bank accounts with overdrafts for everybody is also problematic. This may end up as massive loan waivers which will weaken the banks. If you want to help the poor, give them unconditional transfers out of public revenues, if you like, but not at the expense of the public sector banks' viability.

Q: There are some who say that no-frills accounts for the poor can become viable if there is a move towards direct cash transfers. The earlier government tried but gave up on it. Do you think this is something the new government should push aggressively?

A: We must distinguish between two kinds of cash transfers: transfers to producers and transfers to consumers or citizens. I think producer subsidies such as fertiliser subsidies should be transferred as cash directly to producers. Today, fertiliser subsidies are both regressive, benefiting richer farmers far more than the poor, and inefficient, with a part of the subsidy going to inefficient fertiliser firms.

There will be opposition if you try to reduce such subsidies. So as a first step, the subsidies must be converted to cash transfers, which is somewhat politically easier, and which will make the subsidy transparent. (In this context, if I may be flippant, even the perks and allowances which ministers, MPs and their families receive, such as free flights and transportation and free medical treatment, should all be given in cash, so that you and I know how much each politician costs the country). Transparency will make it easier to reduce such subsidies over time. Even consumer subsidies such as those on LPG (liquefied petroleum gas) cylinders, which benefit mostly the richer sections, should be eliminated. In the case of diesel the subsidy should be eliminated with special vouchers for public buses etc, which the poor use.

Instead, I would favour some kind of universal citizen transfers. Estimates show that total non-merit subsidies funded by both states and the centre amount to roughly 9 per cent of India's Gross Domestic Product (GDP), which largely benefit the better off—the 'dole' for the rich and middle classes. So, I have advocated the following kind of deal: if we can persuade the better-off people to give up only one-third of these subsidies, calculations show that it is possible to provide each household in India, rich or poor, more than Rs 1,000 per month. And you would not even need to raise fresh taxes for this.

Q: So you favour something like a universal basic income?
A: Yes. This is the idea of a universal basic income, and it was originally suggested by some European thinkers in the 19th century (whom Marx called 'utopian socialists'). This is very much on the agenda of green parties in Europe today. This is even more important in India because

we mess up on distinguishing the poor from others. Below Poverty Line (BPL) lists in most states exclude many poor people while many well-off families manage to bribe their way in. Even the *Aadhaar* programme, which I am in favour of, will not solve the problem because the *Aadhaar* card would not tell you if the person is rich or poor. But if you move towards universal transfers, you can avoid the inefficiency and corruption in classifications such as BPL. Of course, mere cash transfers are highly unsatisfactory in case of provision of some basics like healthcare, as the poor are often uninformed about how and where to spend the cash for such basic services. The universal programme I am in favour of in that sector is that of a single-payer universal healthcare system.

Q: You have been involved in a debate on the Mahatma Gandhi National Rural Employment Guarantee Act (MGNREGA). Why do you think the programme should be retained despite leakages?

A: Those of us who support MGNREGA are not saying that there are no problems. Many problems such as delay in payments, corruption, irregularities in materials, etc persist, though there is some evidence that these problems are declining over time in many parts of the country. But despite its problems, it is an effective conditional cash transfer programme. The condition is that you have to work manually to get the transfer, which immediately excludes the middle class and the rich. And it acts as a safety net for the rural poor who find it difficult to get work in the lean season. The sheer existence of an alternative fall-back option improves the bargaining power of landless labourers.

There are leakages, and the programme needs to be improved. But the leakages are very small compared with the subsidies to the rich. The entire programme costs only 0.4 per cent of GDP. Even if you assume that half of it is stolen—which I do not think is true—it still costs only a tiny fraction of the subsidies spent annually on the dole for the rich. So I think there should be some sense of proportion, which people tend to lose, in this debate. There are also those who oppose MGNREGA because they believe it is raising wages but I tell them that any poverty eradication measure will raise the bargaining power of the poor, and hence their wages. If you are against MGNREGA raising wages, you must be consistent and oppose any poverty eradication effort!

So, I am a bit worried about the government's attempts to dilute MGNREGA provisions surreptitiously rather than through openly debated amendments to laws that were passed with the BJP's (Bharatiya Janata Party's) support earlier. The same kinds of changes are happening in case of environmental clearances by means of various 'notifications', a form of reform by stealth (which the Prime Minister publicly says he does not like); similarly, there have been 'notifications' to get rid of the mandated need for consent of local people in the case of deforestation.

Q: What do you think of the 'Make in India' campaign? Do you think India has already missed the manufacturing bus, given that economists such as Dani Rodrik seem to suggest that the days of manufacturing are over?

A: I hope 'Make in India' is not what the *Swadeshi Jagran Manch* used to ask for. If it is about *swadeshi* (of or belonging to one's own country) in another incarnation, then it goes against trade liberalisation. Before trade liberalisation, Indian producers had to use made-in-India intermediate goods, which were sometimes inefficient, rendering finished products costly and uncompetitive. One of the ways in which trade liberalisation improved productivity was that it allowed producers to use more efficient imported materials and components.

As long as it is not in favour of mindless import-substitution, I welcome efforts to boost manufacturing. I do not completely agree with the reported view of Dani

Rodrik that the days of manufacturing are over. Yes, there are some countries where manufacturing has peaked, particularly in exports. But for countries such as India, China, and Indonesia with large domestic markets, there is still a huge scope for manufacturing. Think of the huge increase in demand for light manufactured items when living standards in the rural areas of states such as Odisha, Bihar, Uttar Pradesh (UP), and Madhya Pradesh improve. What is disconcerting is that India is not able to get into even relatively simple manufacturing products in the global value chain that China is getting out of. Countries such as Bangladesh, Vietnam, and Indonesia are ahead of us in making those products.

Q: Are our labour laws to blame for this?
A: The labour regime is a constraint but as I have written earlier, it may not be the binding constraint. I looked at the data on a very labour-intensive industry: garments. Now, if labour laws are the binding constraint, you will expect to find many firms just below the threshold level of 100 workers beyond which stringent labour regulations kick in. But the data do not show that. There is instead bunching at a very low level: at around the eight-employee mark. So, the question really is what prevents an eight-employee firm from becoming an 80-employee firm.

If you ask an eight-employee firm's owner what prevents him from expanding, he is likely to tell you that if he were to expand, and invest in better machines, he will need to assure himself of regular power supply. So, the binding constraint, in my view, may well lie in the poor quality of infrastructure in India, whether it be power, roads, or ports.

China's success in manufacturing is a classic example of infrastructure-led growth. Most people do not know that long before China initiated economic reforms, it had already created the base for an industrial boom by investing heavily in the power sector. Under Mao, China carried out a lot of rural electrification, whereas even today, half of the households in our villages do not use electricity. Of course, China also invested heavily in health and education and that created a much more productive workforce. So in physical and social infrastructure, China had already solved many of its problems much earlier, in the Maoist period.

CHAPTER 12

A Conversation with Amartya Sen

California Magazine, July August 2006

INTRODUCTION[1]

The lives of Amartya Sen, a Nobel prize winner in economics and one of the most celebrated public intellectuals of our time, and Pranab Bardhan, a Berkeley economics professor who specialises in issues of global development and poverty, were marked by coincidence long before they became friends and colleagues. Several years apart, they both spent some of their childhoods in Santiniketan, a Bengali university town famous as the home of the Indian poet and thinker, Rabindranath Tagore. Both attended Presidency College in Calcutta, and they finally met at Cambridge University. Like Bardhan, Sen also taught at Berkeley, arriving in 1964—an intellectually seminal year for him, he says. Beyond economics, Sen and Bardhan share a broad interest in history and culture, perhaps in part, Bardhan suggests, because the Bengali language, which they and more than 200 million others speak, has spawned such a rich literary tradition. *California Magazine* recently reunited the two friends in San Francisco for a discussion of issues

---

1 Introduction by *California Magazine*

raised in Sen's most recent book, *The Argumentative Indian: Writings on Indian History, Culture and Identity*.

Although Sen was primarily awarded the Nobel, in 1998, for highly technical and mathematical advances in social choice theory, he is more widely known as an untiring champion for ending world poverty, for mass education, health care, and women's autonomy, and for promoting democracy and public reasoning, values that he has explicitly linked, notably in his book, *Development as Freedom*. Sen's two recent books, both released within the last year, share a concern with religious and ethnic extremism, and violence.

The Argumentative Indian resurveys Indian history, finding strong traditions of tolerance, scientific and mathematical achievement, and nascent democracy, particularly in the important sense of decision making through public discussion. Sen believes Hindu nationalists (and American "clash of civilisations" theorists) distort India's history with their singular focus on the Hindu tradition, a theme he again takes up in *Identity and Violence*. There he argues that the erroneous and belligerent insistence by religious and ethnic extremists that we have one, true, "discovered" identity—rather than multiple ones that we can reasonably choose among—underlies much of the world's violence.

Pranab Bardhan (PB): Your book, *The Argumentative Indian*, challenges the rather naive interpretation of Indian culture in the West—that analytical reasoning is quintessentially Western, and that Indian culture is primarily concerned with spirituality and uncritical religious faith.

Amartya Sen (AS): That interpretation of Indian culture and civilisation has been dominant in the West's relation with India. When the British were first establishing themselves in the 18th century, people like William Jones and others were quite interested in Indian mathematics and astronomy, and science generally. But by the time the empire settled down, James Mill—who was very proud of the fact that he wrote the history of India without going to India at all, and who also did not speak any Indian language—argued that if there was anything to Indian culture, it is just kind of spiritual, religious stuff. Whereas Jones had discussed important astronomers and mathematicians in ancient India, like Aryabhatta, who rejected the prevailing view of the sun going around the earth.

PB: This is in the sixth century?

AS: He was very late fifth century—his major book was completed in 499 AD. He also discussed diurnal motion of the earth and why is it that objects do not get thrown out into space.

His students and followers, like Varahamihira and Brahmagupta, argued that every object attracted every other—early speculations on gravity. Making India the domain of religion played a part in the undermining of Indian culture. To some extent, India fell into the trap. Rather than contesting that there was quite a strong tradition of science, and also one of atheism and materialism (the earliest atheistic verses you see in the Rig Veda itself, which is around 1500 BC), they said, "Okay, the West is terrific in science, but we are very good in spirituality". It is something quite important to resist.

PB: But the really more dangerous oversimplification about Indian culture and history today is the creation of the Hindu chauvinists in India.

AS: I agree it is dangerous, and a distortion. It is not entirely unrelated to the colonial history. In some ways people had got used to the idea that India was spiritual and religion-oriented. That gave a leg up to the religious interpretation of India, despite the fact that Sanskrit had a larger atheistic literature than exists in any other classical language. Even within the Hindu tradition, there are many people who were atheist. Madhava Acharya, the remarkable 14th century philosopher, wrote this rather great book called *Sarvadarshansamgraha*, which discussed all the religious schools of thought within the Hindu structure. The first chapter is "Atheism"—a very strong presentation of the argument in favour of atheism and materialism. The second chapter is on Buddhism, which is treated as an offshoot of Hinduism. And then it goes through the other schools of Hinduism.

One of the things I tried to argue in *The Argumentative Indian* is that there is a long tradition of philosophical argument. People ask, "Which really reflects Indian culture? Is it this or is it that?" What reflects Indian culture most are the arguments themselves, rather than any resolution in one direction or the other. The Hindu sectarian view of Indian nationalism is based on a historical misinterpretation, and then they distort history by rewriting textbooks. The religious rhetoric is exaggerated to suggest that the dominant religion is all there is in terms of the Indian cultural history. That point of view is very limited, very misleading, and indeed, wrong. Then if you add to it the nastiness of sectarian politics whereby regarding other communities to be either inferior or nasty or having treated Hindus badly in the past, like Muslim conquerors are supposed to have, then you generate needless anger and hostility. Sometimes they try to be quite nasty to other communities, and sometimes pretty violent. Some killings have occurred, especially in Gujarat in 2002 and in Bombay about a decade earlier.

PB: What is your take on cultural relativism?

AS: Where it is most diverting is in the field of relativist ethics. It is argued: How can you criticise other countries because in their context, their ethics is the right one? That view overlooks the immensely constructive possibility of arguments that are used in the context of a debate in one culture but where the argument draws also from another. And it is always been like that, even religion. Buddhism arose in India. It is the only agnostic world religion. But it went out to Japan, China, Korea, all kinds of places from India. In contrast, the purely cultural relativist position would be to ask: What has a Korean or Japanese got to learn from the Indians on Buddhism?

A similar thing can be said today. To say of some practice that is prevalent in some countries, like stoning of adulterous woman in Afghanistan or genital mutilation in North Africa, "Look, that is their practice, you cannot criticise", is ridiculous. That critique may not survive even in Somalia or Afghanistan, provided a free discussion is possible, involving women as well as men, rather than dissidents being threatened or being put in jail. One of the strongest arguments that shows the weakness of the cultural relativist dismissal of dissent is the need that authorities have to put local dissidents in jail for taking a "foreign" point of view.

And there are some strong intellectual arguments for universalism. Just as Chomsky claims that our ability to use certain forms of syntax and language are present in all human beings, similarly there are a number of capacities to think on your own, if you try, that exist among different people.

PB: Some of your critics in India—and there are some, true to the argumentative tradition—have said that in this book you have indulged in the same kind of partisan selection of evidence from history that you find in others. They say that spanning more than 2,000 years, for your point about tolerance and pluralism and the inclusionary view of Indian identity, you choose figures like the Emperor Ashoka in the third century BC, Emperor Akbar of the 16th century, and then Rabindranath Tagore in the 19th/ 20th century. And they say that others could choose historical figures representing the opposite: orthodoxy, intolerance, etc.

AS: I am not claiming that Akbar or Ashoka represent anything like the "essential India". My point is that they represent a very strong perspective that has come up again and again, which includes a lot of tolerance. But of course there is also a long history of extreme intolerance and nastiness. Indian culture has this variety that needs acknowledgement. Since the focus has been so much on the other side, I am using my focus as a correction. I have quite an elaborate discussion of science and mathematics in India. This is not a claim that everyone was a scientist in India. It is a claim that that tradition exists.

When we try to draw on the past, we draw always in a selective basis. When the French and the British and the Americans were drawing on the European past in saying there is a democratic tradition, and they referred to Athens and ancient Greece—over a small number of centuries from sixth, fifth, fourth, third century BC—they were not looking at the Goths and Visigoths and Ostrogoths. Because in the context of the debate on democracy in America in the late 18th or early 19th century, the relevant reference is Athenian democracy. Ostrogoths, Vikings, and in a different way, intolerant masters of the Inquisition are no less "European" than ancient Greeks. Nevertheless, one could say if you are looking for representative Europe, it is not like that.

Looking back on our history, it is not surprising that Gandhi or Nehru would emphasise those parts of the Indian tradition of public reasoning that were particularly relevant for modern India—the first poor country which chose to be an uncompromisingly democratic, multi-party state. I do not think any of them claimed that their focus was the only tradition that existed in India.

This point is worth mentioning because there is a tendency in the West to think of something of which they approve as being a Western thought. Describing Iranian dissidents as "ambassadors of European thought" is to add insult to injury because there is also a history in Iran of democracy going back to the third century BC. And to be told that no, no, no, you are actually implants of John Stuart Mill, misdescribes the nature of Iranian dissidence.

PB: Democracy obviously has been a favourite cause of yours. Another favourite cause has been that of mass education, basic health, and women's rights. When you combine these two sets of causes, one cannot help but notice that there could be a disjuncture, not in the realm of your ideas but in the real world of politics. The conditions of basic health and sanitation and primary and secondary education are simply appalling in India. Yet, the electorate does not penalise politicians when they fail to deliver these services. And the conditions continue to be appalling, election after election.

AS: A very interesting question, Pranab. Let me say three things. First, democracy is basically a permissive system. Some of the issues of deprivation are very easy to seize in terms of media and political opposition. Like famines. Hard to win elections after a famine. It is hard to prevent newspapers writing editorials, unless you censor them, criticising the government if famines occur. So these things get immediately politicised. The rest requires a lot of effort. In India, the gender issue—when I first started working on it, you were one of the first to be involved in that. You wrote this great paper . . . what was it called?

PB: "Life and Death Questions in India."[2]
AS: I think you have had the same experience as I had, the people treating it as your and my amiable eccentricity that we are concerned with the gender issue. But nobody

2 *The Economic and Political Needs*, 1974

thinks like that today. If the Indian Parliament is debating today as to how to ensure that a third of the parliamentarians are women, something has changed— and changed as a result of politics, particularly the women's movement.

One of the things I discuss in *The Argumentative Indian* is that despite the fact that since the economic reforms in 1979 the Chinese have grown economically much faster than India, life expectancy in India has increased about three times as fast as that in China over the last quarter century. The reason for it is not so much that the Indians are getting things right, but that the Chinese are getting things pretty bad. Earlier, because of their left-wing communist commitment to basic health care and basic education, the Chinese did a lot of very good things in terms of spreading public education and health care. Often, the health care was of a very low quality, but nevertheless, there was universal coverage. At the time of the economic reform, the Chinese did away with universal social insurance of health. One morning, simply abolished it. Rather than 100 per cent of the people being covered, 70 per cent, minimally, are not covered by any kind of health insurance today. You cannot imagine in a democratic country an established right of citizens could have been compromised so easily.

On top of that, people publicly grumble in India all the time. Every now and then, that confronts politicians with the need to do something, which the Chinese government does not quite have to face. By not knowing that, for example, SARS had in fact surfaced in November of one year but would not be revealed until the April of the following year, China put things in a closet, which prevents a kind of inescapable improvement that you see in India. So my second point is that the democratic critique is still, even in India, making a difference.

My third point is that democracy is primarily, as I see it, not just voting, but public reasoning, government by discussion. To initiate the discussion is a contribution to democracy. You might not have thought that your "Life and Death Questions" was a contribution to Indian democratic practice, but that is what it was because a lot of people read it and were inspired by it and moved by it.

For years, people used to say every time I gave a lecture, "You are going on and on about democracy, but if democracy is so good, how come India does not grow at all?" My answer was that economic growth depends not on the harshness of the political climate, but the friendliness of the economic climate. People do not ask me that rhetorical question anymore because India's economic growth is quite high now. But the country is no less democratic today—it is not democracy that had to be abandoned to grow fast.

PB: But people do suggest—in the China-India comparison, for example—that your argumentative Indians are merely verbose; there is more talk, less action. They take a long time to come to a decision. In some matters of economic development, you need to make decisions quickly. In 1990, the Chinese did not have any superhighways, and now, in superhighway mileage, they are the second in the world next to the United States. Try to have a highway in India and there will be endless discussion. There will be land disputes, agitations by people who may be uprooted, they will then go to political parties, and some political party will take a position, "No, you cannot do that", etc.

AS: There are certain things that are much easier to do in China. There if you have to uproot people to build a highway, you can build it and not worry too much about their approval. It does not matter what rights they may have. If you want to make the country in such a way that autobahns could be constructed very quickly, or—as Mussolini used to claim, the trains should be run on time— if that is the only value, then I think there is a lot of merit in giving up democracy. But if you take rights of others seriously, if you regard that citizens and their claims to their little space make a difference, then I am afraid the longer route becomes inescapable, no matter if it delays the autobahn or if the train to Rome arrives 25 minutes late. Secondly, quickness of decision is not necessarily the best recipe for good action. The Chinese, with the same rapidity as building superhighways, also abolished the universal insurance of health. In India, that would have been delayed, and would have been stopped. China executes every week more people than India has executed in its entire history since independence 60 years ago. I do not think I want to be the citizen of a country that does things like that. I am happy enough to be a citizen of a country that discusses the rich variety of Chinese experiences in a democratic way and decides that we do want some of these things, but not others.

PB: The culture in which you and I grew up, the Bengali culture, is suffused with the ideas of Tagore, but the rest of the world—and even the rest of India—are more familiar with the ideas of Gandhi. What were their different views of India?

AS: Tagore is, of course, immensely known in Bangladesh and in parts of India in a way that he is not anywhere else in the world. Gandhi, because of politics being a more communicable process, also because of his influence on Martin Luther King and Mandela and others, has a much bigger set of admirers.

They both were extremely keen on a non-sectarian India. I think both would have approved—I flatter myself in thinking—of my project in *The Argumentative Indian*. On the other hand, their traditions were different. Gandhi was much more religious in a traditional sense than Tagore was. Tagore did believe in God, but he was God-respecting, God-loving, again and again describing God as "my friend" as opposed to someone you are really in awe of. With Gandhi, some of the God-fearingness came in. I would put him somewhere between the God-fearing part of Christianity and Tagore's God-loving, which in a sense is a development out of the *Vaishnava* movement in Hinduism, as well as the influence of Sufis that came into India on the Islamic side and led to the kind of harmonious combination in the writings of Kabir and Dadu and others four or five hundred years ago. That kind of religiosity is very important for Tagore. But that is easily combinable with science. Tagore was a great believer in science education; Gandhi was not. Their attitudes toward birth control were quite different. Tagore was in favour of family planning. Gandhi was very much against it. He was in favour of abstinence. Tagore actually has a passage where he comments on the tremendous fear of sex that Gandhiji had. I cannot say that Tagore was a great model of sexual indulgence. His wife died, of course, quite young, but it seems from all accounts that he developed some kind of a crush on a very talented Argentine woman named Victoria Ocampo. And she too fell very much in love with Tagore. But Tagore was very clumsy and tied up in his own thoughts, and it did not really lead to a . . . not only not consummation, but not to any kind of further pursuit of that relation.

PB: He was into his seventies when they became . . .
AS: It began earlier, but Tagore's involvement lasted through his seventies. But now that I have entered the seventies, I do not necessarily accept that there is something clinically wrong in having an involvement! Gandhi, of course, also remained much more of a politician than Tagore. When Tagore and Gandhi were both involved in the anti-untouchability movement in the 1930s, and the Bihar earthquake took place in 1934, in which a lot of people died, Gandhi immediately converted that into a political

advantage by saying that this is God's punishment for untouchability. It seemed like an effective argument. Tagore was appalled by it, both because he thought that introducing politics into a situation in which a lot of the people killed were children who had nothing to do with untouchability was a pretty nasty thing to do. He also thought that earthquakes have scientific causes that people should understand, about the nature of the earth and the tectonic movements. Despite the fact that Gandhi was such a moral person, he was certainly not above using very instrumentally convenient arguments for pursuing a good cause. In that sense, he emerged much more as a consequentialist than he actually, in his theory, ever revealed.

PB: Let us end with some discussion of your new book, *Identity and Violence*. I would like you to relate it to this raging debate that is going on, both in Europe and the United States, on multiculturalism. In Europe, it is raging because they are discussing what to do about the radical Muslims in their midst. But it has come up in this country as well.

AS: The new book is really concerned with the importance of the recognition that we have many different identities, and that violence is often cultivated and fomented in the world—political violence in particular—by denying all identities other than one, one belligerent identity. You are suddenly told you are a Hutu, and Hutus hate Tutsis. And you are a Hutu exclusively. You are not a Rwandan, not an African, not a human being—identities that Tutsis also have. It is by cultivating one single bellicose identity that violence is often fostered. I saw that as a child. You were probably a little too young, but you might have watched a little bit of the aftermath of that, of how the Hindu-Muslim identity suddenly took over from the broader identity as Indian and human being, or neighbour. The book is really about the evil of the illusion of a single identity. The subtitle of the new book is *The Illusion of*

Destiny—the idea that somehow you have one pre-determined identity and that determines what you can do and how you should live. But, in fact, it is up to us to determine what relative importance to attach to our different affiliations. The Rwandan could say that he is a Rwandan and a Kigalian and an African and a human being, just as he can also say, "I am a Hutu".

Not only do terrorists, but also those who want to reduce the prevalence of terrorism, often fall for the same trap. A Muslim person has many identities. A Muslim person may have an Islamic identity. This can be very important if they are religious. But they may also have an identity as a mathematician, identity as a squash player or cricket player, identity as a conservative or a liberal or a radical in politics. Bangladesh separated from Pakistan not on grounds of religion but on grounds of language, literature, culture, and politics, secular politics. But increasingly the battle is engaged by saying, "Yes, the only way of thinking of a Muslim is in terms of Islamic identity", and then to claim, as Prime Minister Tony Blair does, that Islam is a "religion of peace". That is just as much of an overgeneralisation as the terrorists' statement that Islam is a religion that requires you to kill those who are opposed to Islam. There have been Muslim rulers who behaved just as the terrorists suggest. Sultan Mahmoud of Gazni, who raided India a number of times and looted and destroyed temples, killed a lot of people, was certainly a Muslim. But so was Akbar, immensely tolerant, whose codification, I believe, of minority rights and the need for public discussion had a very strong inspiring effect in the construction of Indian secularism, even democracy insofar as democracy is seen as a government by discussion. Both of them were Muslims. They shared a religion but not politics, nor their civic beliefs.

The term "moderate Muslim" is a similar confusion. You are trying to capture in one word the moderateness of politics and moderateness of religion. But, in fact, you could be a very strongly religious Muslim and yet very moderate in politics. At the time when Mahatma Gandhi and Muhammad Ali Jinnah were debating, Gandhi was very keen on keeping religion out of political divisions. But he was deeply religious. Jinnah was very keen that religion—Islam, Hinduism, etc—be brought into politics. But he was not a particularly good Muslim. He ate pork, he drank whiskey, and so on.

The tragedy is that it is not only those who instigate violence, but also those trying to fight that violence, who get imprisoned by that impoverished idea that we have one principal, un-chosen identity over which we have no command. The need for choice and responsibility, along with clarity of ideas, deserves greater recognition. It can even help to build peace.

Index

Technological progress, 15, 50, 127
28, 198
Tectonic movement, 242
Telecommunication spectrum, 45,
60, 67-68, 74, 78, 89, 95
Theocratic-authoritarian regime, 183
Toxic pollution, 23, 42, 134, 143
Trade liberalisation, 5-6, 14, 17, 45,
125, 127, 228
Trade protection, 50
Trade-off, 27, 79, 99, 179, 188, 197,
199
Transnational, 10-12
Transparency International, 25

Under-pricing, 18, 157
Unemployment, 35, 164, 179, 191
Universal citizen transfer, 226
Unorganised sector, 123
Upper-caste, 90, 96-97, 99
Utopian socialist, 226

Vajpayee, Atal Behari, 169

Vikaspurush, 170, 213
Visigoths, 236
Vocational training, 54, 79, 188, 204,
217, 222

W, Yip, 138-40
Washington Consensus, 24, 142
Watchdog, 15, 189, 201
West Bengal, 96-97, 126, 163, 182
186, 189-92, 209, 213
Western Enlightenment, 97
Whyte, Martin, 23
Workforce, 18, 52, 54, 68, 211, 230
World Bank, 5, 10, 17, 21-22, 24-25,
69, 120-21, 126, 136, 190
World Development Report, 13, 126

Xenophobia, 151
Xiaobo, Liu, 146-48
Xiaoping, Deng, 106

Yeats, William Butler, 73
Yew, Lee Kuan, 42